Picture Reference
ATLAS

MEL PICKERING

In association with
FRANKLIN WATTS

Conceived, designed and edited by:
Two-Can Publishing Ltd
346 Old Street
London
EC1V 9NQ

Text: Andrew Solway
Consultant: Steve Watts
Computer illustrations: Mel Pickering, Jacqueline Land
Editors: Deborah Kespert, Kate Asser
Editorial support: Claire Llewellyn, Julia Hillyard, Claire Yude
Art director: Belinda Webster
Senior designer: Helen Holmes

This edition published 1997 by Two-Can Publishing in association with
Franklin Watts
96 Leonard Street
London
EC2A 4RH

Hardback ISBN 1 85434 371 8
Paperback ISBN 1 85434 372 6

2 4 6 8 10 9 7 5 3 1

A catalogue record for this book is available from the British Library.

Photographic credits: Zefa p7, John Englefield p9

Printed and bound in Spain by Graficas Reunidas

Contents

What is an atlas?

An atlas is a book of maps showing different parts of the world. Maps are small pictures of big places drawn from above. They can show somewhere as small as a village or as big as the world. You can use atlases and maps in all sorts of ways. They might show you how to find your way around, or tell you what a place is like.

1 One of the most difficult maps to draw is one showing all of the world. This is because the world is round, like a huge ball, but maps are flat. Imagine painting the world on to the skin of an orange.

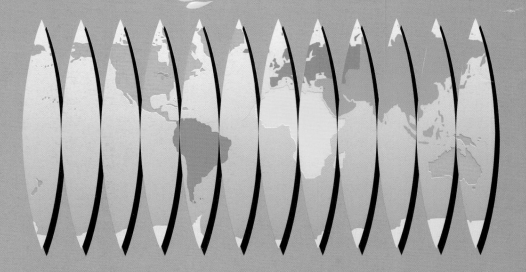

2 You could carefully peel the skin into segments.

3 Then you could lay the peel flat to make a map of the world.

4 Mapmakers fill the gaps by stretching some parts of the map and squashing others.

On this map, you can see that more than half of the Earth is covered by four big oceans. The rest of the Earth is divided into seven huge areas of land, called continents. There are also three imaginary lines on the map. The equator circles the Earth's middle. The Arctic Circle is at the top of the Earth and the Antarctic Circle is at the bottom.

ARCTIC OCEAN

Arctic Circle

NORTH AMERICA

EUROPE

ASIA

PACIFIC OCEAN

ATLANTIC OCEAN

AFRICA

Equator

INDIAN OCEAN

SOUTH AMERICA

AUSTRALIA

Antarctic Circle

ANTARCTICA

Different kinds of maps show different amounts of detail, but most maps show places much smaller than they really are.

1 This is a picture of a house on the corner of Park Street, which runs through a sea-side town. You can see the hedge around the house, the tree outside and some of the street, but you cannot see the town or the sea because the picture is not big enough to show all these details.

2 This map shows Park Street as if drawn from above. It shows less detail but a bigger area than the last picture. Can you spot the house on the corner? On this map, Park Street measures 10cm, but it is really 1km long. This means that on the map every 10cm is the same as 1km in the real place. This is called scale.

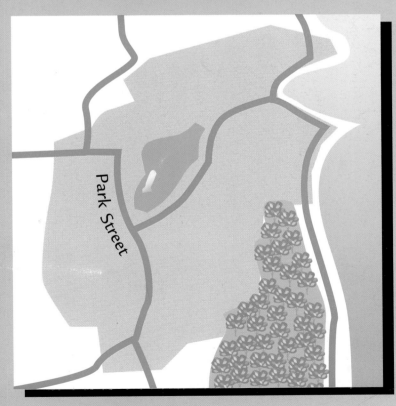

Park Street

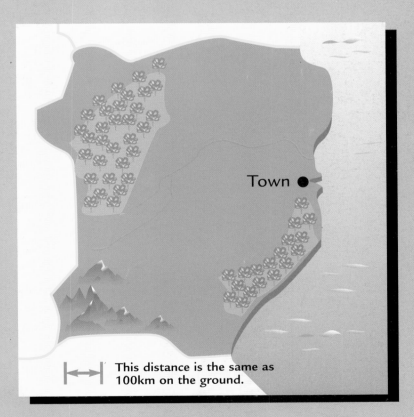

Town ●

This distance is the same as 100km on the ground.

3 This map shows a bigger area than the last map because it has a smaller scale. It shows all of the town. Look how close it is to the sea. You cannot see the houses or all the streets, but you can see Park Street. On this map, Park Street is 5cm long. This means every 5cm on the map is the same as 1km in the real place.

4 This map shows the country where the town is found. Now the town is only shown by a black dot. The scale bar tells you that 1cm on the map is the same as 100km in the real place. In this atlas, each map has a different scale and scale bar. On pages 10-11 you can see all the countries of the world at the same scale.

Hot and cold

Around the world, there are different patterns of weather called climates. The climate of a country depends on where it is in the world. It is always hot near the equator and cold near the North and South Poles. On each map in this atlas, you will find a locator globe, showing you where countries and continents are in the world. The globe has arrows pointing to the four directions – north, south, east and west.

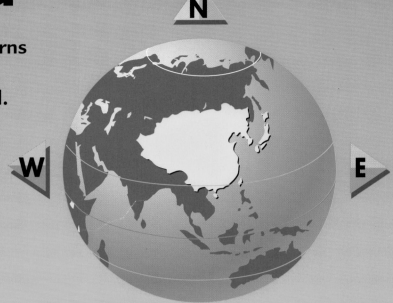

The sun warms all the countries in the world, but shines more strongly on some than others. These countries have the warmest weather. Around the world, the weather also changes at different times of year.

Arctic Circle

Tropic of Cancer

Equator

Tropic of Capricorn

Around the North and South Poles, the sun is never high in the sky and shines weakly, so the land is always cold, especially in winter.

Near the equator, the sun shines strongest and directly from above. Here the climate is hot, with wet and dry seasons.

Above and below the equator, there are two imaginary lines called the Tropic of Cancer and the Tropic of Capricorn. Countries between the tropics and the North and South Poles have warm summers and cold winters.

Different climates suit particular kinds of plants, and make different types of land for animals and people to live in. If a place has a rainy climate, lots of plants grow. If the climate is dry, fewer and different plants grow.

On the map below and the maps in this atlas, different types of land are shown by small pictures, called symbols, and colours. These photographs show you what the land really looks like.

Usually, the poles are icy cold. In summer, a few small plants grow around the Arctic.

Deciduous forests grow in cool areas. The trees lose their leaves in autumn.

Evergreen trees stay green all year. Evergreen forests grow in cold places.

Grassland includes tropical savannah (seen here), farmland and flat plains, called pampas.

Only the toughest plants and animals are able to survive in dry deserts.

Thick, green rainforests grow where it is warm and wet all year.

Few plants grow on rocky mountains, which are often covered in snow.

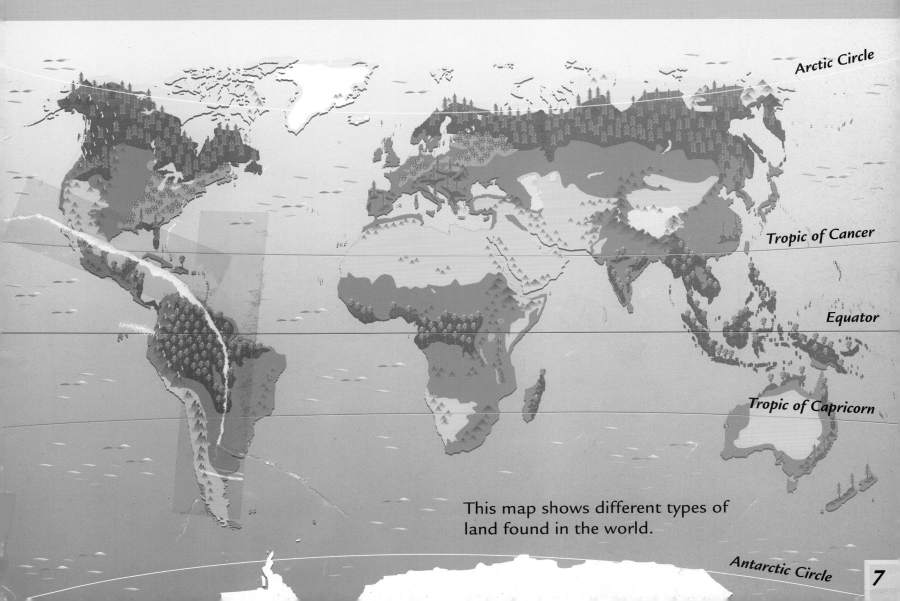

Arctic Circle

Tropic of Cancer

Equator

Tropic of Capricorn

This map shows different types of land found in the world.

Antarctic Circle

About this atlas

The maps in this atlas can tell you an enormous amount about the places they show. Look carefully at the pictures to find out more.

Crops grow all over the world. Look out for wheat, rice, fruit and vegetables. You may see coffee, tea and sugar cane, too.

Each country is run from a capital city. These are shown by the flag of the country and a star.

Some buildings are shown on the maps. You may see a famous monument, an old ruin or a type of home.

A grey line shows a country border. When countries are arguing about a border or are not sure where the border is, the line is dotted.

This picture shows where people drill into the land and seabed for oil, which is used to power all kinds of machines.

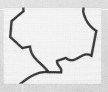
A blue line shows a river. The name of the river is written alongside. Rivers can run through many countries.

Different kinds of animals live in different parts of the world. Look for animals that live in the sea, on land and in the air.

Royal gramma fish

This picture shows where people mine for diamonds. People also mine coal, silver, jewels, gold, copper, tin and iron.

Oil

VENEZUELA

Rice

Rice

Cayenne

GUYANA
Georgetown

SURINAM
Paramaribo

FRENCH GUIANA (France)

Different people live around the world. Look for people playing sport or enjoying a traditional dance.

Diamonds

Gold

Angel Falls

Equator

Gold

Crocodile

Emerald tree boa

Piranha fish

Gold

Cargo ships

Dug-out canoes

Tobacco

Sugar cane

River Amazon

B R A Z I L

Cotton

Oil

Toucan

Recife

Diamonds

Umbrella bird

Stilt house

Gold

Sloth

Rainforest clearing

Oil

Shrimp

Jaguar

Vampire bat

River São Francisco

Gold

Corn

Iron

Cotton

Sugar cane

Gold

Brasília

Tourism

Lobster

BOLIVIA

Oil

Gold

Rice

Oranges

Cotton

Wheat

La Paz

Cotton

Gas

Cotton

Iron

ANDES MOUNTAINS

Potatoes

Cattle ranching

Carnival

About the Factfile

Each map has a Factfile with facts about the places you can see. You might find out about a special animal or plant from a particular part of the world. Look at the picture beside each fact and then find it on the map. The facts in this Factfile are about the map of part of South America shown on the opposite page. Can you find all the pictures on the map?

On page 42, you will find a gazetteer, full of all different kinds of facts about the countries of the world.

Factfile

South America is home to nearly one quarter of all known animals and around 2,500 different kinds of trees.

The longest mountain range in the world is the Andes in South America.

Half of all the people in South America live in Brazil.

FACT FINDER

Each map has a grid, which divides it into squares. The columns run up and down and have letters. The rows run from side to side and have numbers. This means each square has a name, or grid reference.

The Fact Finder asks questions about places on the map. You can find the answers by looking at the grid reference.

Here is a Fact Finder question about the map of part of South America shown on the opposite page.

▶ What is the name of the highest waterfall in the world? (See square E 4.)

To find square E 4, lay your ruler on column E, at the bottom of the map. Leave the ruler lying on the map. Now put your finger on row 4, at the side of the map. Run your finger along row 4 in a straight line. Square E 4 is where your finger meets the ruler.

You should have found Angel Falls which is in Venezuela.

▼ This girl is answering the Fact Finder question. She is using a ruler and her finger to find the correct grid reference.

World map

ALASKA (USA)

GREENLAND
(Denmark)

ARCTIC
OCEAN

FINLAND   NORWAY

ICELAND

THE
NETHERLANDS

SWEDEN
ESTONIA
LATVIA

CANADA

UNITED
KINGDOM

These
countries in
Europe are
shown more
clearly inside
the circle on
page 11.

REPUBLIC
OF IRELAND

BELGIUM

ATLANTIC
OCEAN

FRANCE

ANDORRA

UNITED STATES
OF AMERICA

SPAIN

PORTUGAL

BALEARIC
ISLANDS
(Spain)

MALTA

AZORES
(Portugal)

TUNISIA

CRETE
(Greece)

BERMUDA (UK)

MADEIRA
(Portugal)

MOROCCO

DOMINICAN REPUBLIC
PUERTO RICO (USA)
VIRGIN ISLANDS (USA & UK)
ANGUILLA (UK)
ST KITTS & NEVIS
ANTIGUA & BARBUDA
GUADELOUPE (France)
DOMINICA
MARTINIQUE (France)
ST LUCIA
BARBADOS
GRENADA
TRINIDAD & TOBAGO

CANARY
ISLANDS
(Spain)

ALGERIA

LIBYA

MEXICO

BAHAMAS

WESTERN
SAHARA

BELIZE

CUBA

CAPE
VERDE
ISLANDS

MAURITANIA

MALI

NIGER

CHAD

JAMAICA

GUATEMALA

HONDURAS   HAITI

MONTSERRAT (UK)

SENEGAL

EL SALVADOR

NICARAGUA

ST VINCENT &
THE GRENADINES

GAMBIA

GUINEA-
BISSAU   GUINEA

BURKINA
FASO

NIGERIA

CENTRAL
AFRICAN
REPUBLIC

COSTA RICA

PANAMA

VENEZUELA

GUYANA

SIERRA
LEONE

IVORY
COAST

GHANA

BENIN

TOGO

CAMEROON

GALAPAGOS
ISLANDS
(Ecuador)

COLOMBIA

SURINAM

FRENCH
GUIANA
(France)

LIBERIA

SÃO TOMÉ & PRÍNCIPE

GABON

ECUADOR

EQUATORIAL
GUINEA

CONGO

ZAIRE

PERU

BRAZIL

CABINDA
(Angola)

ANGOLA

PACIFIC
OCEAN

ZAMBIA

BOLIVIA

NAMIBIA

PARAGUAY

BOTSWANA

The world is divided into
almost 200 countries and
this map shows most of
them. The countries are
different colours so that
you can tell them apart.
Some countries own places
in other parts of the world.
In this atlas, these kinds of
places have two labels. One
label gives their name and another
label in brackets gives the name of
the country that owns them.

ATLANTIC
OCEAN

REPUBLIC OF
SOUTH AFRICA

CHILE

URUGUAY

LESOTHO

ARGENTINA

FALKLAND
ISLANDS
(UK)

SOUTH
GEORGIA
(UK)

ANTARCTICA

RUSSIA

KAZAKHSTAN

AZERBAIJAN

UKRAINE

ARMENIA

GEORGIA

TURKEY

CYPRUS

SYRIA

LEBANON

IRAQ

JORDAN

ISRAEL

EGYPT

SAUDI
ARABIA

SUDAN

ERITREA   YEMEN

DJIBOUTI

ETHIOPIA

SOMALIA

UGANDA

KENYA

RWANDA

BURUNDI

TANZANIA

MALAWI

COMOROS

MAYOTTE (France)

ZIMBABWE

MOZAMBIQUE

SWAZILAND

MADAGASCAR

UZBEKISTAN

TURKMENISTAN

KYRGYZSTAN

TAJIKISTAN

AFGHANISTAN

IRAN

KUWAIT

BAHRAIN

QATAR

UNITED
ARAB
EMIRATES

OMAN

PAKISTAN

NEPAL

INDIA

MONGOLIA

CHINA

BHUTAN

MYANMAR

BANGLADESH

LAOS

THAILAND

VIETNAM

CAMBODIA

ANDAMAN
ISLANDS
(India)

NICOBAR
ISLANDS
(India)

SOCOTRA
(Yemen)

MALDIVE
ISLANDS

SRI
LANKA

SEYCHELLES

NORTH
KOREA

JAPAN

SOUTH
KOREA

MACAU
(Portugal)

TAIWAN
(China)

HONG
KONG
(UK)

PHILIPPINES

BRUNEI

MALAYSIA

SINGAPORE

INDONESIA

IRIAN JAYA
(Indonesia)

PAPUA NEW
GUINEA

PACIFIC
OCEAN

NORTHERN
MARIANAS
(USA)

GUAM (USA)

MARSHALL
ISLANDS

PALAU
(USA)

STATES OF MICRONESIA

NAURU

KIRIBATI

TUVALU

SOLOMON
ISLANDS

INDIAN
OCEAN

AUSTRALIA

TASMANIA
(Australia)

VANUATU

FIJI

NEW
CALEDONIA
(France)

NEW ZEALAND

SWEDEN

LATVIA

LITHUANIA

(Russia)

DENMARK

BELARUS

GERMANY

POLAND

LUXEMBOURG

CZECH
REPUBLIC

SLOVAKIA

UKRAINE

LIECHTENSTEIN

AUSTRIA

MOLDOVA

HUNGARY

SWITZERLAND

SLOVENIA

ROMANIA

CROATIA

FEDERAL
REPUBLIC OF
YUGOSLAVIA

MONACO

SAN
MARINO

BOSNIA-
HERZEGOVINA

BULGARIA

CORSICA
(France)

ITALY

MACEDONIA

TURKEY

ALBANIA

SARDINIA
(Italy)

VATICAN
CITY

GREECE

SICILY
(Italy)

Some countries in Europe are
crowded together. In this circle,
we have made these countries
bigger so that you can see
them more easily.

11

The Arctic

The Arctic is the part of the world that lies closest to the North Pole. Around the Pole, the Arctic Ocean is frozen all year, but further away the ice and snow melt in the summer. In winter, the sun hardly shines which makes the Arctic very cold. Very little grows there, except for a few small plants such as moss or lichen.

FACT FINDER

▶ Which Arctic animal weighs more than nine grown men and lives on the moving ice? (See square F 8.)

▶ Which bird travels further than any other bird in the world? Every year it flies over 13,000km from the North to the South Pole? (See square F 7.)

▶ What do Arctic peoples often use to travel across the ice? (See E 8.)

Factfile

The largest group of people in the Arctic are the Inuit. They have lived there for thousands of years.

The first person to travel to the North Pole from outside the Arctic was the American explorer, Robert Peary, in 1901.

The edge of the Arctic Ocean is one of the world's richest areas for fishing.

This distance is the same as 1,900km on the ground.

Antarctica

Antarctica is an enormous ice-covered continent near the South Pole. It is the coldest and windiest place on Earth. Few animals live around the pole but there are seals and birds on the coast, and plants and fish in the sea. The only people living in Antarctica are scientists. They stay on research stations to study the land and its wildlife.

Factfile

In 1911, Roald Amundsen, a Norwegian explorer, became the first person to reach the South Pole.

Up to 30,000 tourists a year cruise the waters around Antarctica to see the land and its wildlife.

Antarctica has many icebergs. The largest one ever found was three times the size of the island of Cyprus.

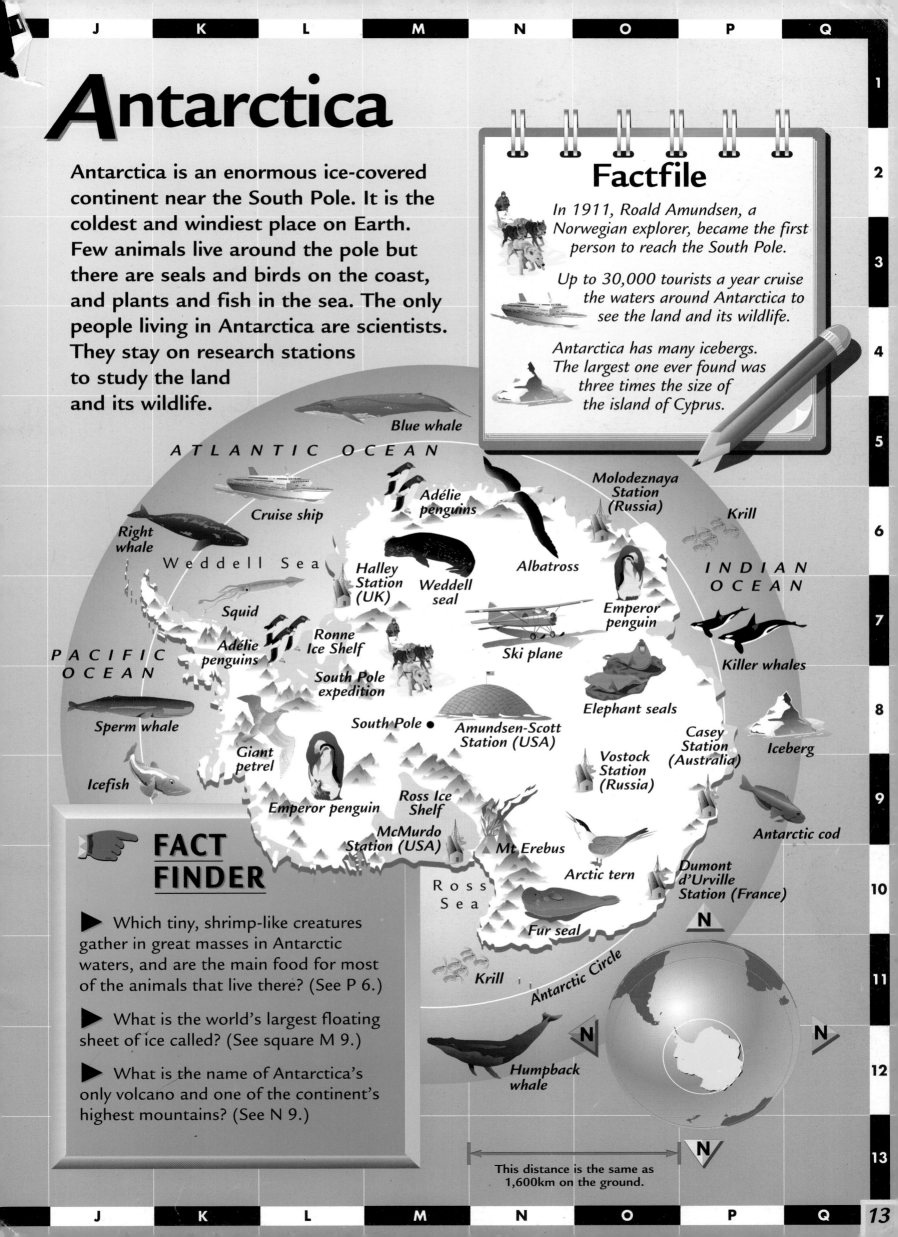

Blue whale · ATLANTIC OCEAN · Cruise ship · Adélie penguins · Molodeznaya Station (Russia) · Krill · Right whale · Weddell Sea · Halley Station (UK) · Weddell seal · Albatross · INDIAN OCEAN · Squid · Emperor penguin · Adélie penguins · Ronne Ice Shelf · Ski plane · Killer whales · PACIFIC OCEAN · South Pole expedition · Elephant seals · Casey Station (Australia) · Iceberg · Sperm whale · South Pole · Amundsen-Scott Station (USA) · Vostock Station (Russia) · Giant petrel · Antarctic cod · Emperor penguin · Ross Ice Shelf · McMurdo Station (USA) · Mt Erebus · Dumont d'Urville Station (France) · Arctic tern · Ross Sea · Fur seal · Krill · Antarctic Circle · Humpback whale

FACT FINDER

▶ Which tiny, shrimp-like creatures gather in great masses in Antarctic waters, and are the main food for most of the animals that live there? (See P 6.)

▶ What is the world's largest floating sheet of ice called? (See square M 9.)

▶ What is the name of Antarctica's only volcano and one of the continent's highest mountains? (See N 9.)

This distance is the same as 1,600km on the ground.

Canada

Canada is the second biggest country in the world after Russia. Large parts of it are cold and empty. In the north, there are huge pine forests and the weather is often freezing. Most people live in the south where it is warmer. Canada produces oil and mines coal, silver, gold and copper. It has good farmland, where farmers grow enormous fields of wheat. It also has large factories, mostly in the east, that make and sell goods, such as cars, trucks and trains.

ARCTIC OCEAN

Ice breakers

Arctic tern

Parry Islands

Killer whales

Banks Island

Musk ox

Victoria Island

ALASKA

Canadian Royal Mounted Police

Salmon

Oil

Husky dogs

River Mackenzie

Great Bear Lake

Silver

Arctic foxes

Mt Logan

YUKON TERRITORY

River Yukon

NORTHWEST

Tourism

Silver

Mountain goat

Wolf

Gas

Gold

Arctic hare

Great Slave Lake

Oil

Indian carvings

ROCKY MOUNTAINS

Bald eagle

Brown bear

Black bear

N

W

E

S

PACIFIC OCEAN

Herring

Gas

ALBERTA

Tourism

Ice hockey

Forestry

Forestry

Grizzly bear

Coal

SASKATCHEWAN

BRITISH COLUMBIA

Edmonton

Apples

Oil

Wheat

Buffalo

Vancouver

Barley

Pronghorn antelope

Oil

Wheat

Ski-ing

Wheat

FACT FINDER

▶ Which game is played using a puck and stick on a large ice rink, and is the country's most popular sport? (See square F 9.)

▶ Which large animal once roamed in huge herds over Canada's grasslands but now lives mostly in national parks? (See square H 10.)

▶ Canada has two main languages, English and French. In which province, or district, would you find most of the French speakers? (See square N 9.)

UNITED STATES OF AMERICA

This distance is the same as 800km on the ground.

14

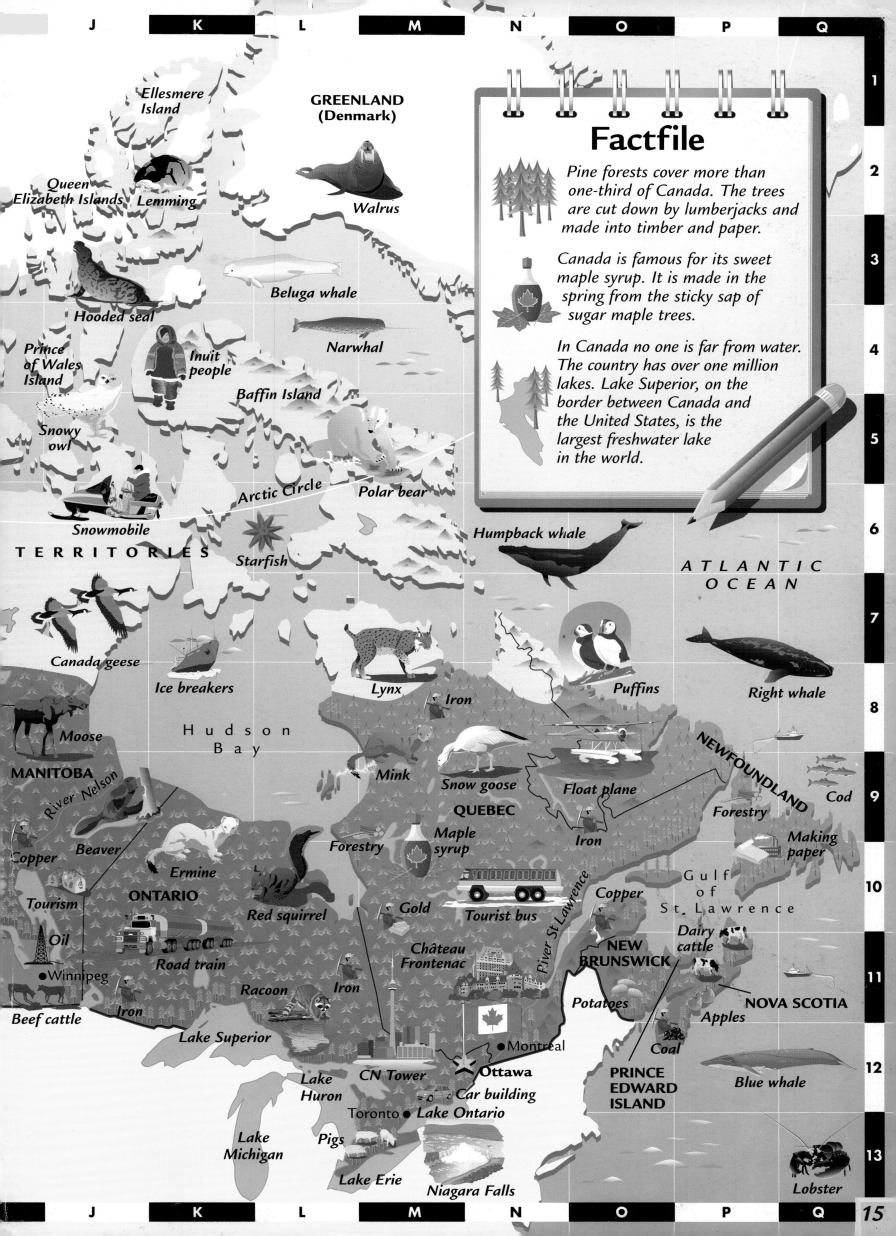

Ellesmere Island

GREENLAND (Denmark)

Queen Elizabeth Islands

Lemming

Walrus

Hooded seal

Beluga whale

Narwhal

Prince of Wales Island

Inuit people

Baffin Island

Snowy owl

Snowmobile

Arctic Circle

Polar bear

Factfile

Pine forests cover more than one-third of Canada. The trees are cut down by lumberjacks and made into timber and paper.

Canada is famous for its sweet maple syrup. It is made in the spring from the sticky sap of sugar maple trees.

In Canada no one is far from water. The country has over one million lakes. Lake Superior, on the border between Canada and the United States, is the largest freshwater lake in the world.

Humpback whale

T E R R I T O R I E S

Starfish

A T L A N T I C O C E A N

Canada geese

Ice breakers

Lynx

Iron

Puffins

Right whale

Moose

H u d s o n B a y

Mink

Snow goose

Float plane

NEWFOUNDLAND

Cod

MANITOBA

River Nelson

QUEBEC

Iron

Forestry

Copper

Beaver

Forestry

Maple syrup

Making paper

Ermine

ONTARIO

Red squirrel

Gold

Tourist bus

River St Lawrence

Copper

G u l f o f S t. L a w r e n c e

Dairy cattle

Tourism

Oil

Château Frontenac

NEW BRUNSWICK

●Winnipeg

Road train

Racoon

Iron

Potatoes

NOVA SCOTIA

Beef cattle

Iron

Lake Superior

CN Tower

●Montreal

Apples

Coal

PRINCE EDWARD ISLAND

Blue whale

Lake Huron

Car building

Ottawa

Toronto ● Lake Ontario

Pigs

Lake Michigan

Lake Erie

Niagara Falls

Lobster

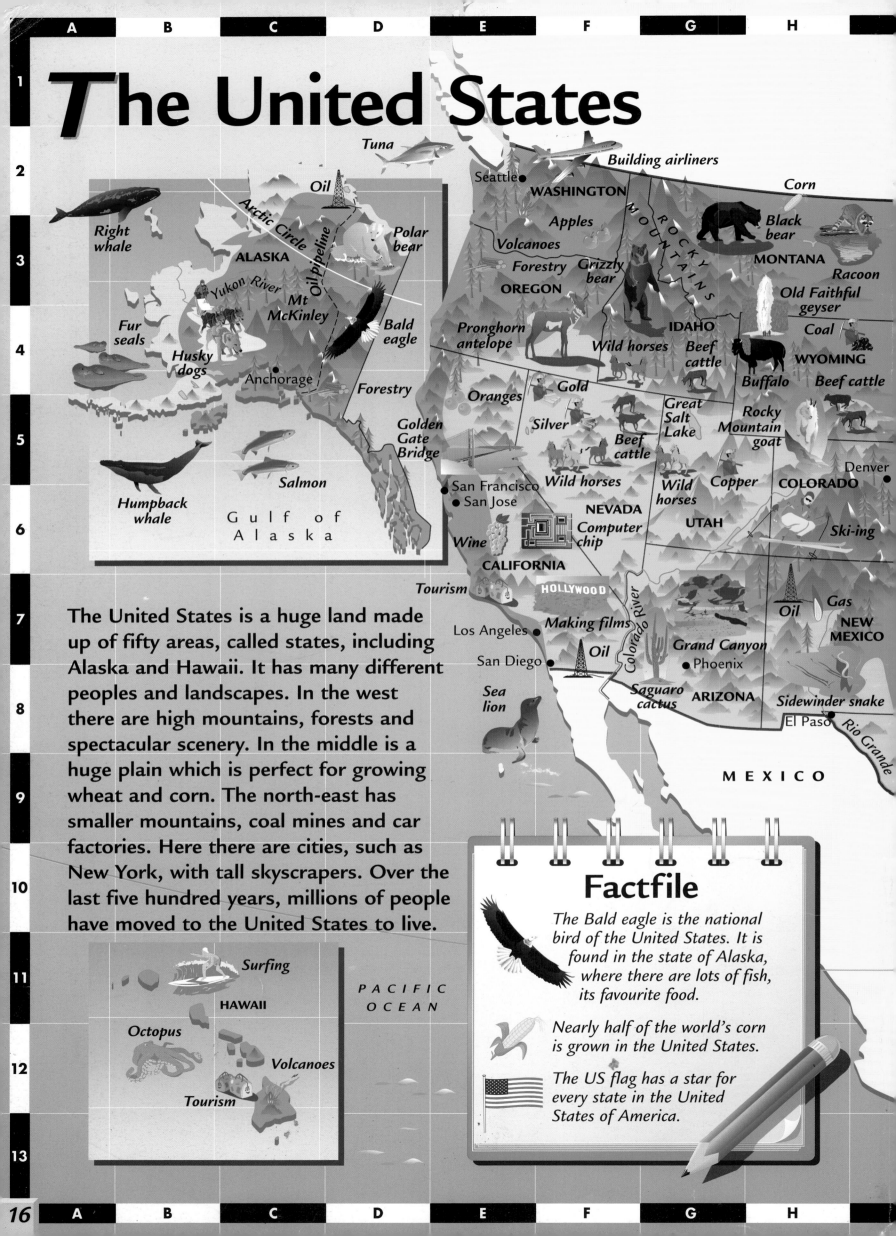

The United States

The United States is a huge land made up of fifty areas, called states, including Alaska and Hawaii. It has many different peoples and landscapes. In the west there are high mountains, forests and spectacular scenery. In the middle is a huge plain which is perfect for growing wheat and corn. The north-east has smaller mountains, coal mines and car factories. Here there are cities, such as New York, with tall skyscrapers. Over the last five hundred years, millions of people have moved to the United States to live.

Factfile

The Bald eagle is the national bird of the United States. It is found in the state of Alaska, where there are lots of fish, its favourite food.

Nearly half of the world's corn is grown in the United States.

The US flag has a star for every state in the United States of America.

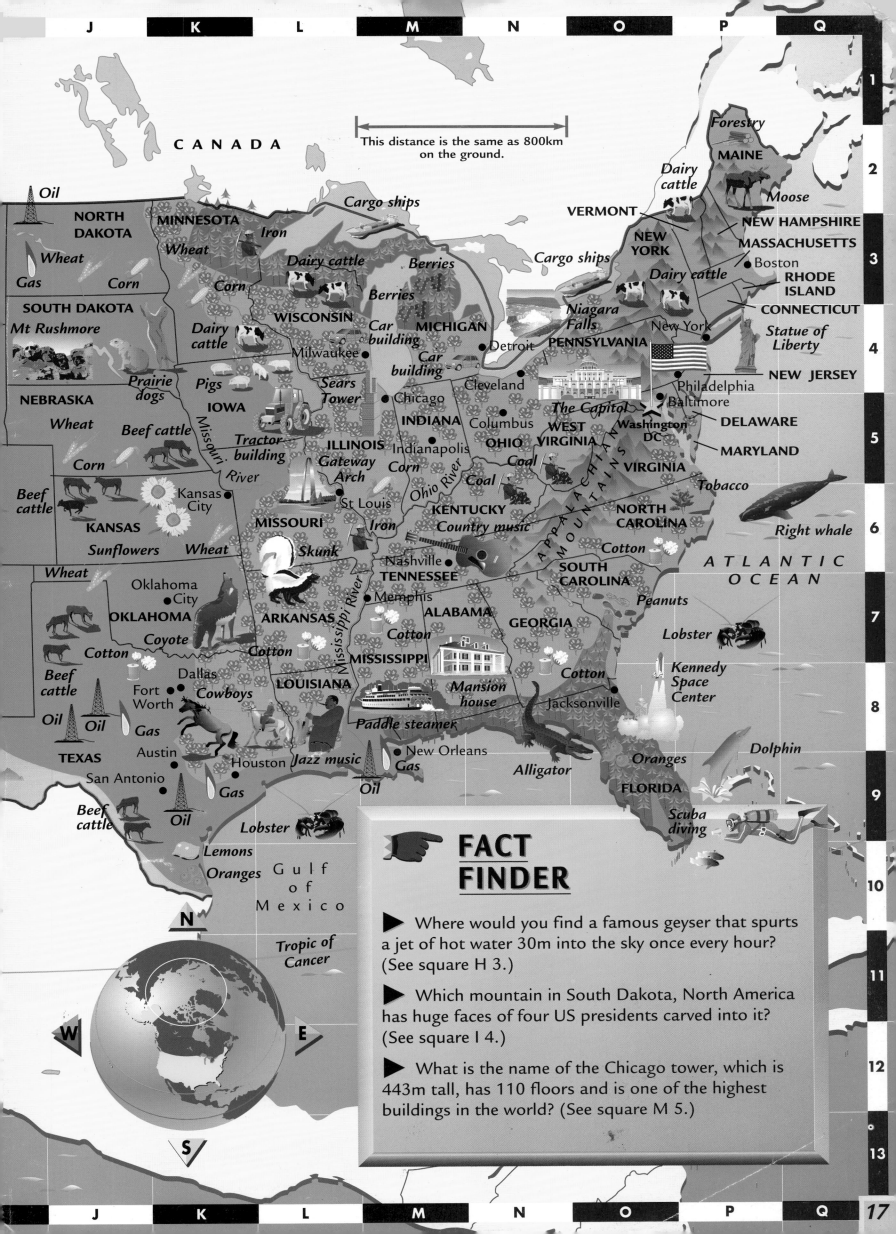

CANADA

This distance is the same as 800km on the ground.

Oil

NORTH DAKOTA

MINNESOTA

Cargo ships

Iron

Wheat

Wheat

Gas

Corn

Corn

Dairy cattle

Berries

SOUTH DAKOTA

Berries

Mt Rushmore

Dairy cattle

WISCONSIN

Car building

MICHIGAN

Forestry

MAINE

Dairy cattle

Moose

VERMONT

NEW HAMPSHIRE

NEW YORK

MASSACHUSETTS

Boston

Cargo ships

Dairy cattle

RHODE ISLAND

CONNECTICUT

Milwaukee

Car building

Niagara Falls

New York

Statue of Liberty

Prairie dogs

Pigs

IOWA

Sears Tower

Detroit

Cleveland

Chicago

PENNSYLVANIA

The Capitol

Washington DC

NEW JERSEY

Philadelphia

Baltimore

DELAWARE

NEBRASKA

Wheat

Beef cattle

Missouri River

Tractor building

ILLINOIS

Gateway Arch

Indianapolis

INDIANA

Corn

OHIO

Columbus

WEST VIRGINIA

Coal

MARYLAND

VIRGINIA

Corn

Beef cattle

St Louis

Ohio River

Coal

Tobacco

Kansas City

MISSOURI

KENTUCKY

Country music

NORTH CAROLINA

Right whale

KANSAS

Skunk

Iron

Nashville

Cotton

ATLANTIC OCEAN

Sunflowers

Wheat

TENNESSEE

SOUTH CAROLINA

Wheat

Oklahoma City

Memphis

ALABAMA

GEORGIA

Peanuts

OKLAHOMA

Coyote

ARKANSAS

Cotton

Lobster

Cotton

Cotton

MISSISSIPPI

Mansion house

Kennedy Space Center

Beef cattle

Dallas

Cowboys

Cotton

Oil

Oil

Fort Worth

Gas

LOUISIANA

Paddle steamer

Jacksonville

Austin

Houston

Jazz music

New Orleans

Alligator

Oranges

Dolphin

TEXAS

San Antonio

Gas

Gas

Oil

FLORIDA

Oil

Beef cattle

Lobster

Scuba diving

Lemons

Oranges

Gulf of Mexico

N

W   E

S

Tropic of Cancer

FACT FINDER

▶ Where would you find a famous geyser that spurts a jet of hot water 30m into the sky once every hour? (See square H 3.)

▶ Which mountain in South Dakota, North America has huge faces of four US presidents carved into it? (See square I 4.)

▶ What is the name of the Chicago tower, which is 443m tall, has 110 floors and is one of the highest buildings in the world? (See square M 5.)

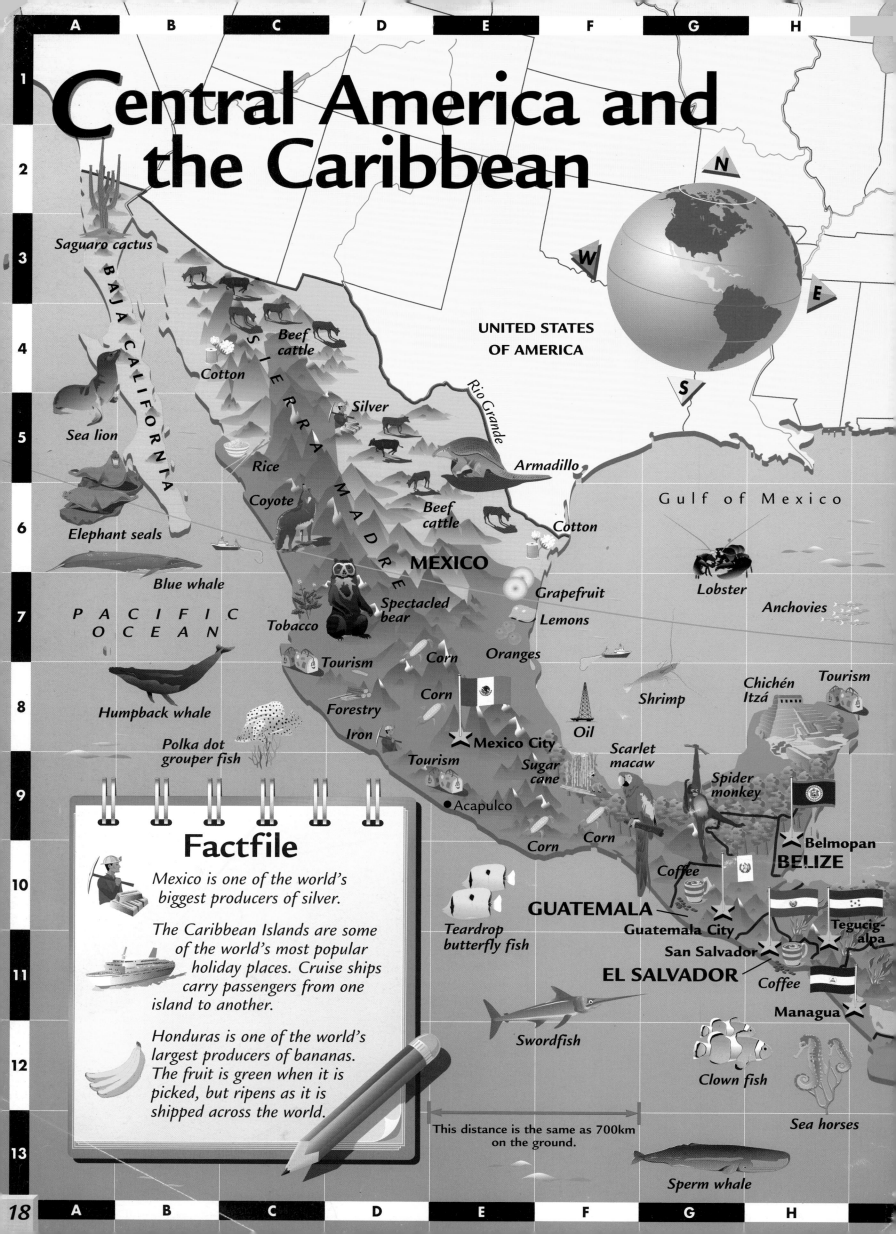

Central America and the Caribbean

UNITED STATES OF AMERICA

N
W
E
S

Saguaro cactus

Beef cattle

Cotton

Silver

BAJA CALIFORNIA

SIERRA MADRE

Sea lion

Rice

Coyote

Elephant seals

Rio Grande

Armadillo

Beef cattle

Gulf of Mexico

Cotton

Blue whale

PACIFIC OCEAN

MEXICO

Lobster

Anchovies

Grapefruit

Lemons

Spectacled bear

Tobacco

Oranges

Corn

Shrimp

Chichén Itzá

Tourism

Humpback whale

Tourism

Corn

Forestry

Iron

Oil

Scarlet macaw

Spider monkey

Polka dot grouper fish

Mexico City

Tourism

Sugar cane

Corn

Corn

Belmopan
BELIZE

• Acapulco

Coffee

Factfile

Mexico is one of the world's biggest producers of silver.

The Caribbean Islands are some of the world's most popular holiday places. Cruise ships carry passengers from one island to another.

Honduras is one of the world's largest producers of bananas. The fruit is green when it is picked, but ripens as it is shipped across the world.

GUATEMALA

Teardrop butterfly fish

Guatemala City

Tegucig- alpa

San Salvador

EL SALVADOR

Coffee

Swordfish

Managua

Clown fish

This distance is the same as 700km on the ground.

Sea horses

Sperm whale

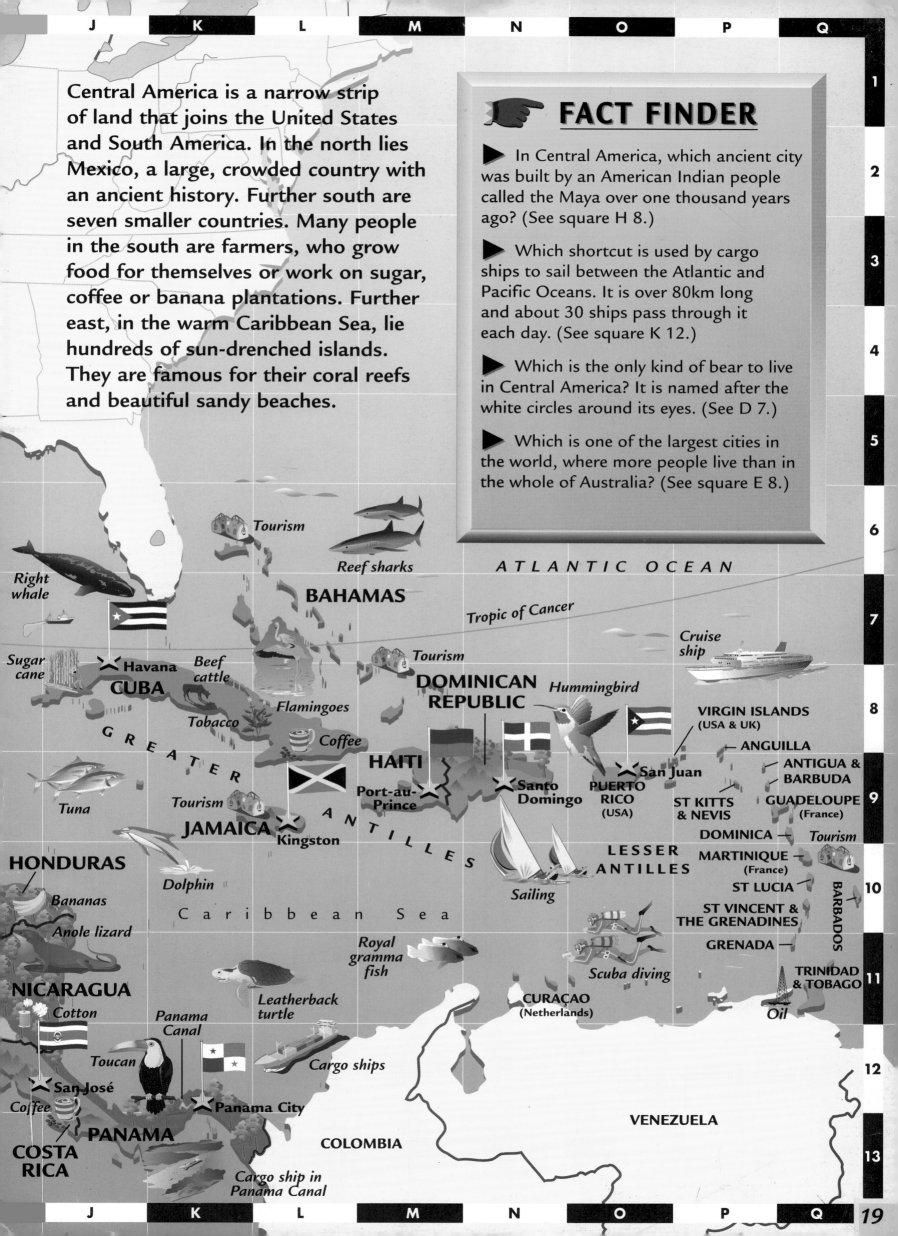

Central America is a narrow strip of land that joins the United States and South America. In the north lies Mexico, a large, crowded country with an ancient history. Further south are seven smaller countries. Many people in the south are farmers, who grow food for themselves or work on sugar, coffee or banana plantations. Further east, in the warm Caribbean Sea, lie hundreds of sun-drenched islands. They are famous for their coral reefs and beautiful sandy beaches.

FACT FINDER

▶ In Central America, which ancient city was built by an American Indian people called the Maya over one thousand years ago? (See square H 8.)

▶ Which shortcut is used by cargo ships to sail between the Atlantic and Pacific Oceans. It is over 80km long and about 30 ships pass through it each day. (See square K 12.)

▶ Which is the only kind of bear to live in Central America? It is named after the white circles around its eyes. (See D 7.)

▶ Which is one of the largest cities in the world, where more people live than in the whole of Australia? (See square E 8.)

Tourism

Reef sharks

ATLANTIC OCEAN

Right whale

BAHAMAS

Tropic of Cancer

Cruise ship

Sugar cane

Havana

Beef cattle

Tourism

CUBA

DOMINICAN REPUBLIC

Hummingbird

VIRGIN ISLANDS
(USA & UK)

Flamingoes

Tobacco

Coffee

HAITI

Santo Domingo

San Juan

ANGUILLA

G R E A T E R

Port-au-Prince

PUERTO RICO
(USA)

ANTIGUA & BARBUDA

Tuna

Tourism

ST KITTS & NEVIS

GUADELOUPE
(France)

JAMAICA

A N T I L L E S

Kingston

DOMINICA

Tourism

HONDURAS

Dolphin

LESSER ANTILLES

MARTINIQUE
(France)

BARBADOS

Bananas

C a r i b b e a n   S e a

Sailing

ST LUCIA

Anole lizard

ST VINCENT & THE GRENADINES

Royal gramma fish

GRENADA

Scuba diving

TRINIDAD & TOBAGO

NICARAGUA

Leatherback turtle

CURAÇAO
(Netherlands)

Cotton

Panama Canal

Oil

Toucan

Cargo ships

San José

Panama City

Coffee

PANAMA

COLOMBIA

VENEZUELA

COSTA RICA

Cargo ship in Panama Canal

South America

The continent of South America stretches from the warm Caribbean Sea to the stormy waters around Cape Horn. South America is warm all year, except in the far south and in the high Andes Mountains. In the north, the great River Amazon flows through tropical rainforest. Further south, there are flat plains where millions of cattle graze. Most South Americans live in cities on the coast. In the country, the farmers grow bananas, coffee beans and corn.

Factfile

South America is home to nearly one quarter of all known animals and around 2,500 different kinds of trees.

The longest mountain range in the world is the Andes in South America.

Half of all the people in South America live in Brazil.

👉 FACT FINDER

▲ Which South American river flows into over 200 smaller rivers to cover an area of land almost as big as Australia? (See square F 5.)

▲ Which Brazilian city holds a world-famous carnival about forty days before Easter every year? (See square L 8.)

▲ What is the name of South America's smallest independent country? (See square G 3.)

▲ Which desert in Chile contains the driest place in the world, where it may not rain for four hundred years? (See square E 9.)

▲ Which South American tree has a sap that people can drink? (See square D 3.)

This distance is the same as 900km on the ground.

N S E W

GALAPAGOS ISLANDS (Ecuador)

Giant tortoise

Tourism

Sardines

Tropic of Capricorn

Humpback whale

PACIFIC OCEAN

PARAGUAY

Asunción

Sheep Wheat Llama Cotton Pigs Rice

Beef cattle Iron Tourism

Car... ...to São Paulo building

Cargo ships

Rice Sheep Coal Beef cattle

URUGUAY Montevideo

Office blocks

ATLANTIC OCEAN

Right whale

River Paraná

ARGENTINA Buenos Aires

Cattle ranching

Sugar cane Cattle ranching Pigs Tourism

ANDES MOUNTAINS

Atacama Desert

Gold Oil Copper Wine Tourism

Santiago

Apples Coal

CHILE

Mt Aconcagua Ski-ing Volcanoes Apples

Armadillo

Andean condor

Beef cattle Gas Oil

Dolphin

Elephant seals

FALKLAND ISLANDS (UK)

Gentoo penguins

Sheep Oil

Tierra del Fuego

Cape Horn

Sheep

Fur seal

Cargo ships

21

Northern Europe

Northern Europe is a cool part of the world where it can rain all year round. It has mountains and pine forests in the far north, and higher mountains in the south. In between lies flat land that was once covered by forest. Over hundreds of years, the trees have been cleared to make room for farms, towns and cities. Most northern Europeans live in towns and work in factories, shops and offices.

Narwhal

Puffins

Arctic Circle

ICELAND
Strokkur geyser

Reykjavík

Sheep

Arctic tern

Viking longship remains

Trondheim

Ski-ing
Mt Glittertinden

Gas

Oil

Shetland pony

Bergen

Oil Gas

Making paper

Oslo

NORWAY

Cod

ATLANTIC OCEAN

Osprey

Herring

Cod

Ship building

NORTHERN IRELAND (UK)

Red deer

North Sea

Dairy cattle

Salmon

Edinburgh

Belfast

Car building

Gas

Pigs

REPUBLIC OF IRELAND

Stoat

Oil

DENMARK
Copenhagen

Thresher shark

UNITED KINGDOM

Dublin

Potatoes

THE NETHERLANDS

Pigs

Ship building

Dairy cattle

Sheep

Clogs

Dairy cattle

River Elbe

Harbour porpoise

Badger

Cardiff

Amsterdam

Otters

Starfish

London

Windmills

Hedgehog

Wild ponies

Stonehenge

BELGIUM

GERMANY

Lobster

Channel Tunnel

Brussels

Car building

Tourism

LUXEMBOURG

Coal

Cheese

Eiffel Tower

Chocolate

Frankfurt

Paris

Luxembourg

Forestry

This distance is the same as 480km on the ground.

River Loire

Wine

River Seine

River Rhine

Wine

Woodpecker

Neuschwanstein castle

Wine

FRANCE

Grey heron

LIECHTENSTEIN

Bay of Biscay

Wine

Bordeaux

High-speed trains

River Rhône

Bern

ALPS

Watches

SWITZERLAND

Ski-ing

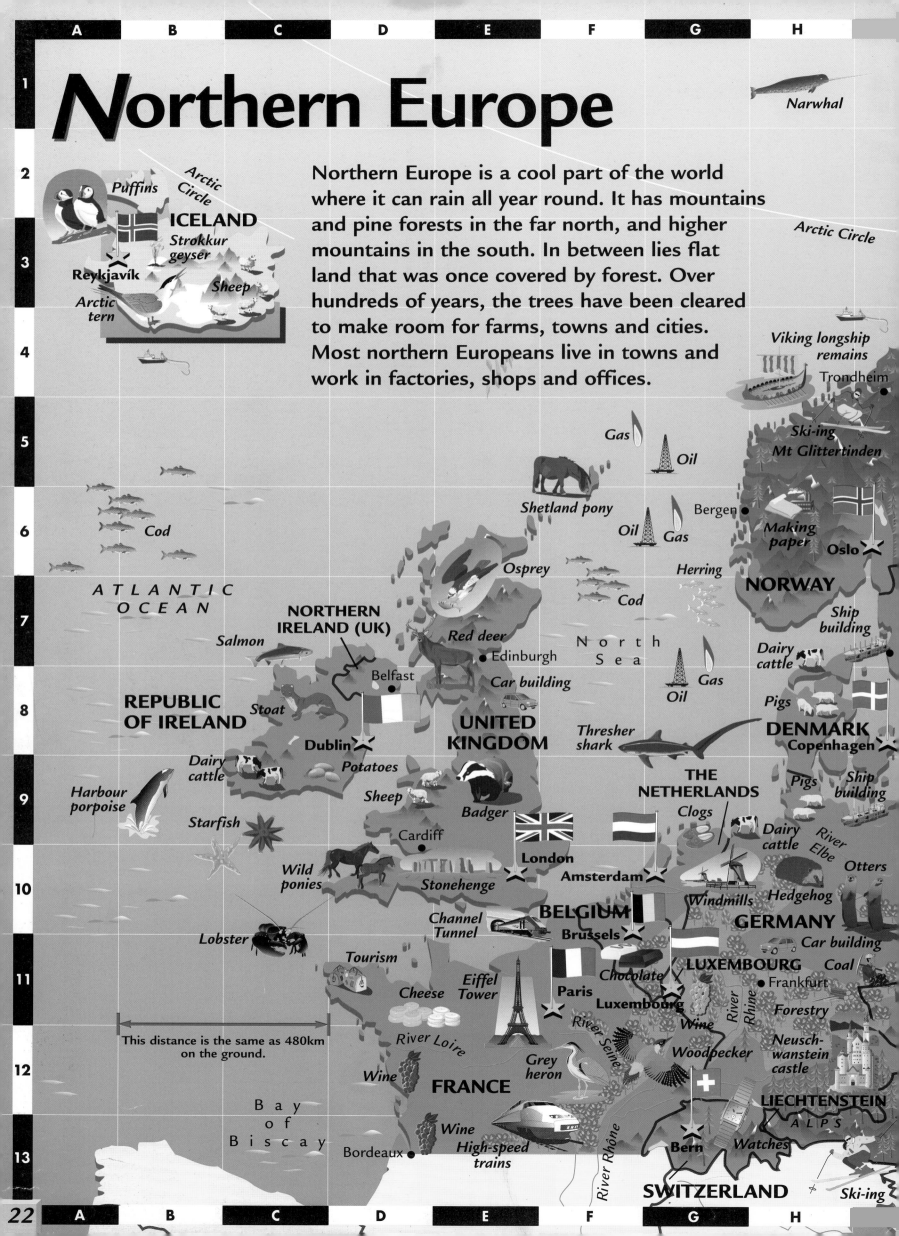

Norwegian Sea

KJØLEN MOUNTAINS

Lapland

Reindeer

Sami people

Iron

Forestry

Lynx

Cross-country ski-ing

Forestry

Forestry

FINLAND

Forestry

Making paper

Making paper

SWEDEN

Salmon

Herring

Helsinki

Fox

Ice breakers

Tallinn

Stockholm

Pigs

ESTONIA

Car building

Building trains

Göteborg

Dairy cattle

LATVIA

Riga

B a l t i c   S e a

LITHUANIA

Malmö

Vilnius

Ship building

Kaliningrad (Russia)

BELARUS

Ship building

Dairy cattle

Potatoes

Red squirrel

Chaffinch

Berlin

Warsaw

Wild boar

POLAND

Coal

Wolf

Prague

Chamois

UKRAINE

CZECH REPUBLIC

SLOVAKIA

Vienna

River Danube

Bratislava

Parliament building

AUSTRIA

Peregrine falcon

Budapest

ROMANIA

HUNGARY

Wild horses

FACT FINDER

▶ Which tunnel in northern Europe is nearly 50km long and allows 400 trains to pass along it in each direction every day? (See square E 10.)

▶ In which country could you see a longship on display, which was built by the Viking people hundreds of years ago? (See square H 4.)

▶ Which famous European tower is 320m high and has 1,652 steps that take you to the top? (See square E 11.)

▶ Which stone monument in England was built around 3,500 years ago, but nobody knows what it was used for? (See square E 10.)

RUSSIA

N

W   E

S

Factfile

There are twice as many pigs in Denmark as people. Two out of three pigs are exported as Danish bacon.

France is visited by more tourists each year than any other country in the world.

Finland produces enough paper to make 5 million comics every day.

Southern Europe

Tourism

BELGIUM

LUXEMBOURG

Tourism

Cheese

Starfish

Cod

ATLANTIC OCEAN

Lobster

Anchovies

Thresher shark

Harbour porpoise

Eiffel Tower

Car building

Paris

River Seine

Champagne

Potatoes

River Loire

Wine

Grey heron

FRANCE

Pigs

High-speed train

Dairy cattle

SWITZERLAND

Beef cattle

Lyon

Roe deer

Milan

Wine

Sheep

Turin

Car building

Genoa

Ship building

ALPS

Beef cattle *Iron*

Potatoes

Wheat

Wolf

Ski-ing

Peregrine falcon

Building airliners

Flamingoes

Tourism

MONACO

Wild horses

Porto

Bullfighter

PORTUGAL

Wheat

ANDORRA

Marseille

Sagrada Familia Cathedral

Cargo ships

Olives

Sheep

Car building

Madrid

Barcelona

CORSICA (France)

Sheep

Lisbon

Windmill

River Tagus

Sheep

Oranges

Anchovies

Sailing

Squid

Iron

Golden eagle

Sheep

SPAIN

Olives

Lemons

Iron

MAJORCA (Spain)

MINORCA (Spain)

SARDINIA (Italy)

Sunflowers

Lynx

Seville

Avocet

IBIZA (Spain)

Wine

Tourism

Lobster

Tourism

Sheep

Wine

Scuba diving

Flamenco dancers

Ski-ing

Tourism

GIBRALTAR (UK)

Anchovies

Mediterranean Sea

Southern Europe is warm, sunny and mainly dry. Large parts of it are covered with mountains and hills, but there is still plenty of good farmland. Many people in southern Europe are farmers. They grow cereals and all kinds of fruit and vegetables. Southern Europe also has many famous ancient buildings and works of art. Each year millions of tourists visit its museums and art galleries.

FACT FINDER

▶ Which Italian bell tower, built over 300 years ago, began to lean before it was even finished? (See square I 6.)

▶ What is the name of the ancient Roman stadium where gladiators once fought with swords and nets? (See J 7.)

▶ Which ancient Greek temple was built to worship the goddess Athene, protector of Athens? (See square N 8.)

POLAND

UKRAINE

GERMANY

N

W

E

S

This distance is the same as 400km
on the ground.

CZECH
REPUBLIC

Ski-ing

Potatoes

MOLDOVA

AUSTRIA

Sheep

Forestry

Red
squirrel

Wolf

Wheat

Making clothes

ROMANIA

Wine

Chamois

HUNGARY

Tractor
building

Sheep

Tobacco

Pizza
Tourism

Ljubljana

Zagreb

Bucharest

Pelican

Venice

SLOVENIA

Olives

River
Po

CROATIA

Oil

B l a c k

Ship
building

Brown bear

Belgrade

S e a

Making
clothes

BOSNIA-
HERZEGOVINA

Gas

River Danube

SAN MARINO

FEDERAL
REPUBLIC OF
YUGOSLAVIA

BULGARIA

Sunflowers

Leaning Tower
of Pisa

Sarajevo

Ponte Vecchio,
Florence

Wild
boar

Dubrovnik

Sofia

Tractor
building

TURKEY

ITALY

Octopus

Istanbul

Vatican
City

Beef cattle

Skopje

Rome

MACEDONIA

Olives

The
Colosseum

Mt
Vesuvius

Tiranë

Goats

Tobacco

TURKEY

Naples

Olives

ALBANIA

Tobacco

Wine

Mt Olympus

Tobacco

Sardines

GREECE

Swordfish

Wine

Squid

The Parthenon

Coot

Tourism

Tuna

Wheat

Palermo

Oranges

Athens

Tourism

Lemons

Olives

SICILY

Cargo ships

Tourism

(Italy)

Mt Etna

Octopus

Oranges

Wine

Tourism

MALTA

Olives

CRETE (Greece)

Factfile

Mount Etna in Sicily is the largest
volcano in Europe. It last erupted
in 1995.

Ship building

Tuna

Squid

Spain produces more olive oil than
any other country. Each year it
produces enough olive oil to
fill 160 Olympic-sized
swimming pools.

Anchovies

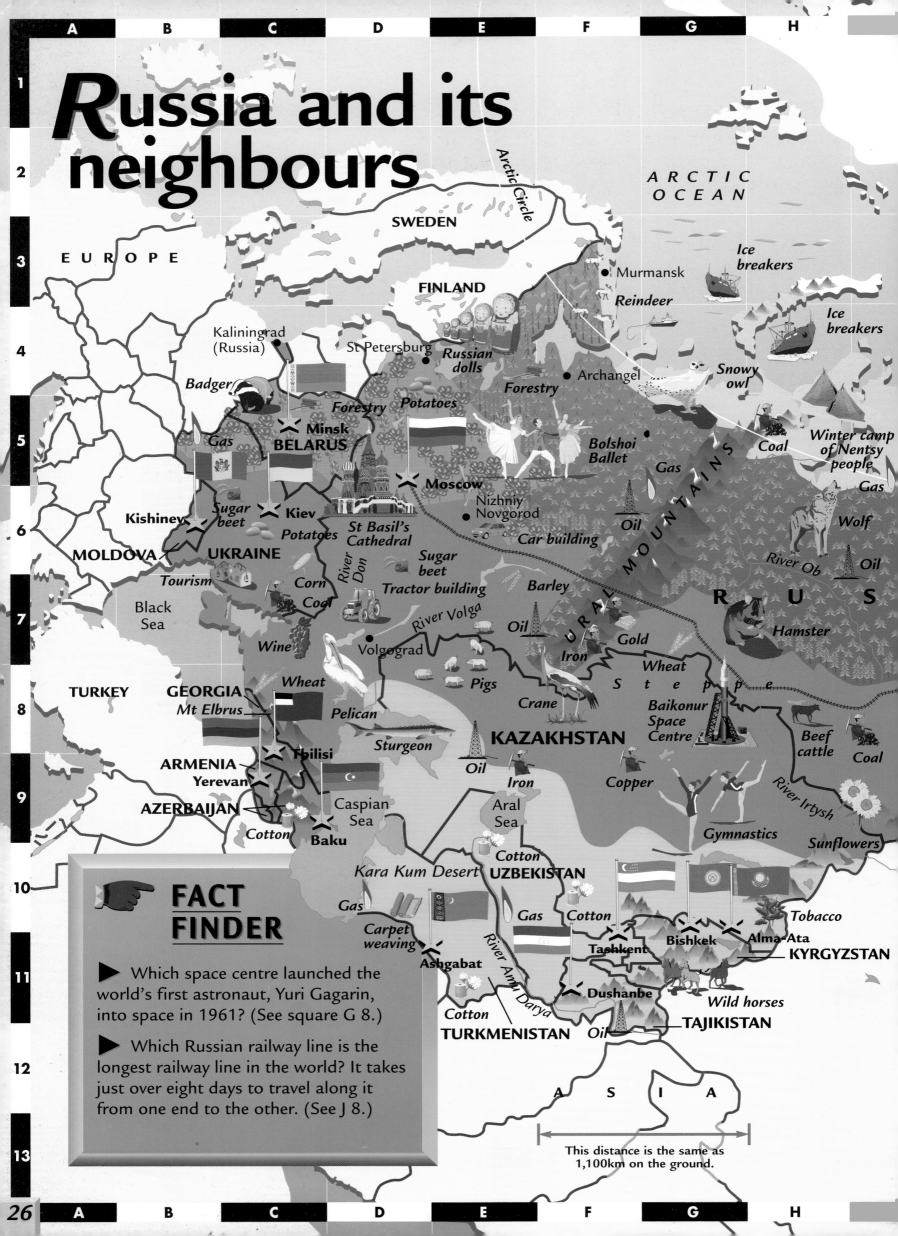

Russia and its neighbours

FACT FINDER

▶ Which space centre launched the world's first astronaut, Yuri Gagarin, into space in 1961? (See square G 8.)

▶ Which Russian railway line is the longest railway line in the world? It takes just over eight days to travel along it from one end to the other. (See J 8.)

This distance is the same as 1,100km on the ground.

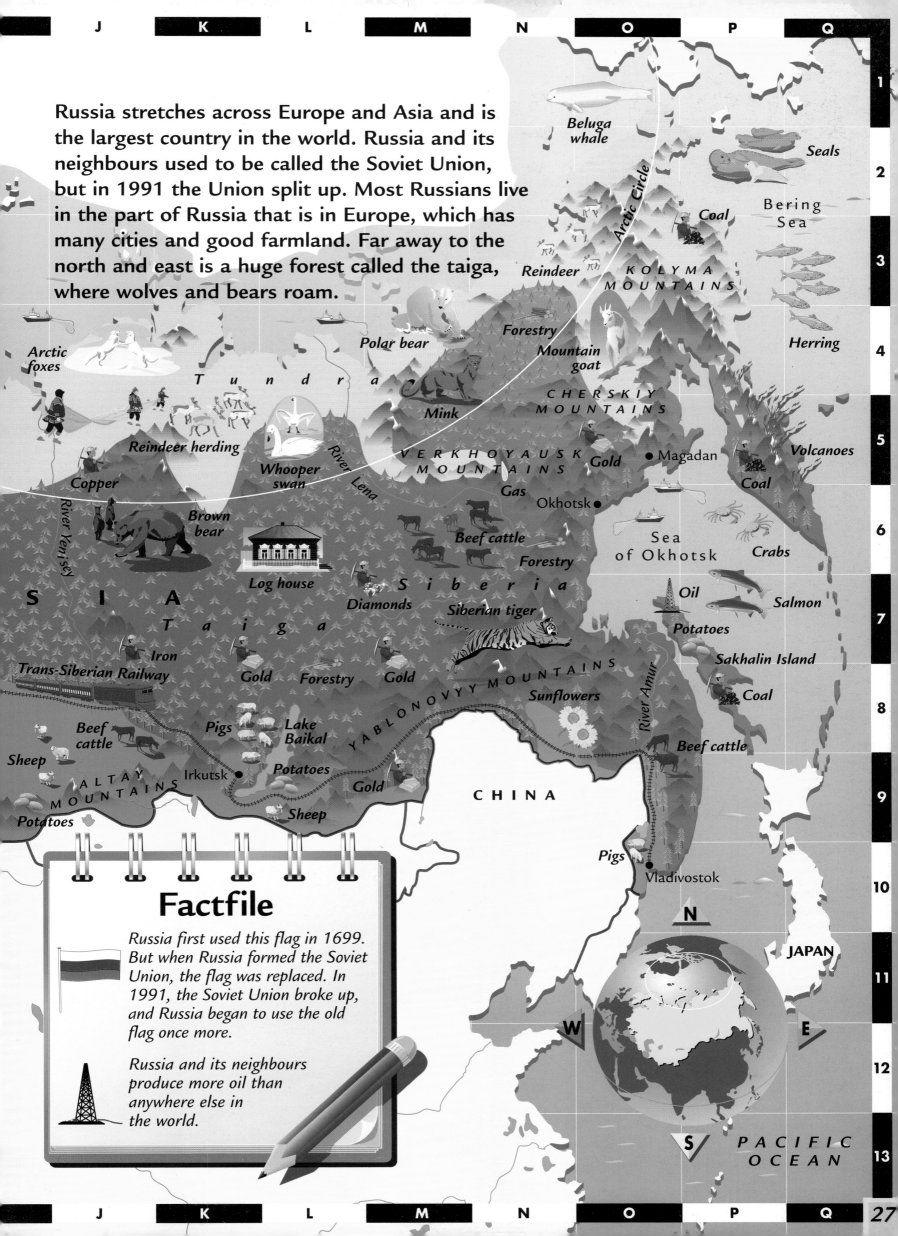

Russia stretches across Europe and Asia and is the largest country in the world. Russia and its neighbours used to be called the Soviet Union, but in 1991 the Union split up. Most Russians live in the part of Russia that is in Europe, which has many cities and good farmland. Far away to the north and east is a huge forest called the taiga, where wolves and bears roam.

Factfile

Russia first used this flag in 1699. But when Russia formed the Soviet Union, the flag was replaced. In 1991, the Soviet Union broke up, and Russia began to use the old flag once more.

Russia and its neighbours produce more oil than anywhere else in the world.

South-west Asia

The south-west corner of Asia is also called the Middle East. Here, thousands of years ago, people first became farmers, then settled close together in towns. Much of the land in south-west Asia is hot, dry desert, which can be hard to farm. Fifty years ago, people found oil under the desert. They used the money they made from the oil to build huge watering systems, so they could grow crops more easily in the poor soil. They also built large cities.

Factfile

Over 5,000 years ago, the first cities in the world grew up in south-west Asia, along the Tigris and Euphrates Rivers.

Three of the world's major religions began in south-west Asia. They are Islam, Judaism and Christianity.

South-west Asia makes some of the world's most expensive hand-made carpets. Carpet-makers weave and knot wool to make different patterns which can tell you the area the carpet comes from.

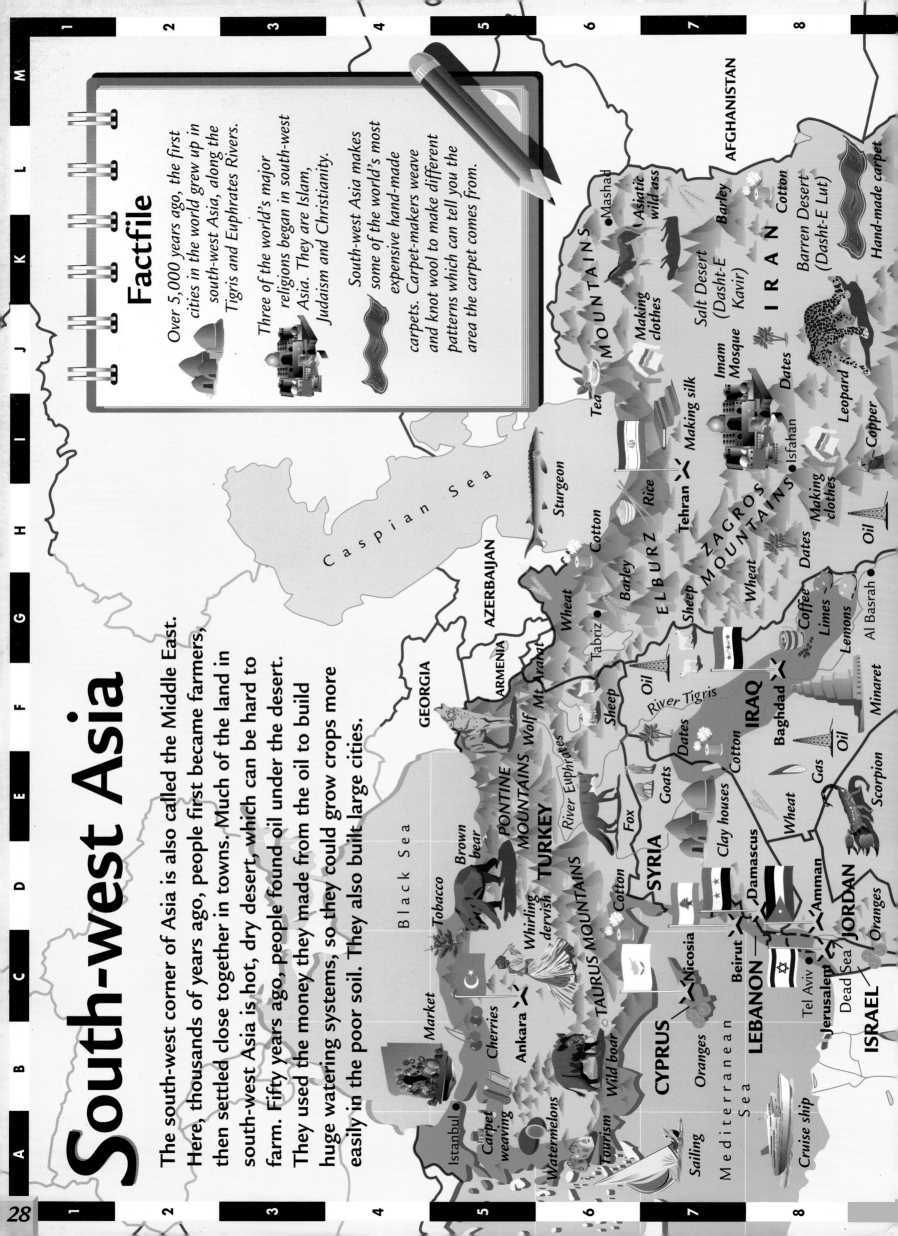

Black Sea

Caspian Sea

Mediterranean Sea

Dead Sea

GEORGIA

ARMENIA

AZERBAIJAN

TURKEY

CYPRUS

LEBANON

ISRAEL

JORDAN

SYRIA

IRAQ

IRAN

AFGHANISTAN

Istanbul

Ankara

Nicosia

Beirut

Tel Aviv

Jerusalem

Amman

Damascus

Baghdad

Al Basrah

Tabriz

Tehran

Isfahan

Mashad

PONTINE MOUNTAINS

TAURUS MOUNTAINS

ELBURZ MOUNTAINS

ZAGROS MOUNTAINS

Mt Ararat

River Euphrates

River Tigris

Salt Desert (Dasht-E Kavir)

Barren Desert (Dasht-E Lut)

Carpet weaving

Watermelons

Tourism

Sailing

Cruise ship

Oranges

Oranges

Wild boar

Cherries

Market

Tobacco

Brown bear

Whirling dervish

Wolf

Fox

Cotton

Clay houses

Goats

Sheep

Sheep

Sheep

Wheat

Wheat

Wheat

Barley

Barley

Cotton

Cotton

Cotton

Cotton

Dates

Dates

Dates

Dates

Oil

Oil

Oil

Oil

Gas

Scorpion

Minaret

Coffee

Limes

Lemons

Rice

Tea

Sturgeon

Making silk

Making clothes

Making clothes

Imam Mosque

Leopard

Copper

Asiatic wild ass

Hand-made carpet

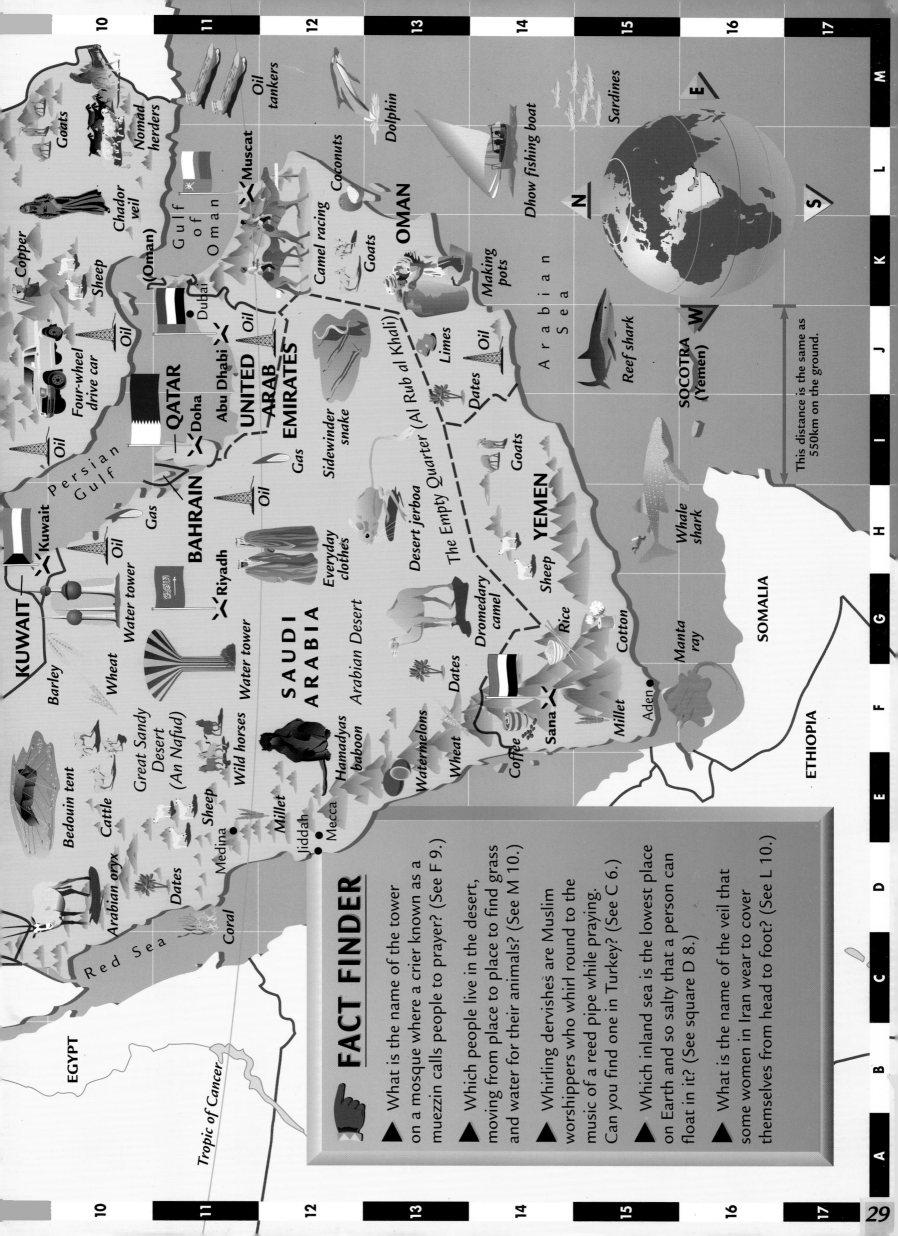

FACT FINDER

▲ What is the name of the tower on a mosque where a crier known as a muezzin calls people to prayer? (See F 9.)

▲ Which people live in the desert, moving from place to place to find grass and water for their animals? (See M 10.)

▲ Whirling dervishes are Muslim worshippers who whirl round to the music of a reed pipe while praying. Can you find one in Turkey? (See C 6.)

▲ Which inland sea is the lowest place on Earth and so salty that a person can float in it? (See square D 8.)

▲ What is the name of the veil that some women in Iran wear to cover themselves from head to foot? (See L 10.)

EGYPT

Tropic of Cancer

Red Sea

Coral

Dates

Arabian oryx

Medina

Jiddah
Mecca

Bedouin tent

Cattle

Sheep

Millet

Watermelons

Wheat

Great Sandy Desert (An Nafud)

Wild horses

Water tower

Hamadyas baboon

Barley

Wheat

Water tower

S A U D I
A R A B I A

Arabian Desert

Dates

Coffee

Sana

Rice

Millet

Cotton

Aden

Manta ray

SOMALIA

ETHIOPIA

KUWAIT

Kuwait

Oil

Gas

Water tower

Oil

Oil

Gas

BAHRAIN

Riyadh

Everyday clothes

Dromedary camel

Sheep

Goats

Y E M E N

Whale shark

Persian Gulf

QATAR
Doha

Oil

Abu Dhabi

UNITED
ARAB
EMIRATES

Oil

Sidewinder snake

Desert jerboa

The Empty Quarter (Al Rub al Khali)

Limes

Dates

Oil

Goats

Making pots

A r a b i a n   S e a

Reef shark

Four-wheel drive car

Oil

Dubai

Gulf
of
Oman

(Oman)

Muscat

Camel racing

Goats

OMAN

Dolphin

Coconuts

Dhow fishing boat

Sardines

Oil tankers

Nomad herders

Goats

Sheep

Chador veil

Copper

N

W

S

E

SOCOTRA (Yemen)

This distance is the same as 550km on the ground.

29

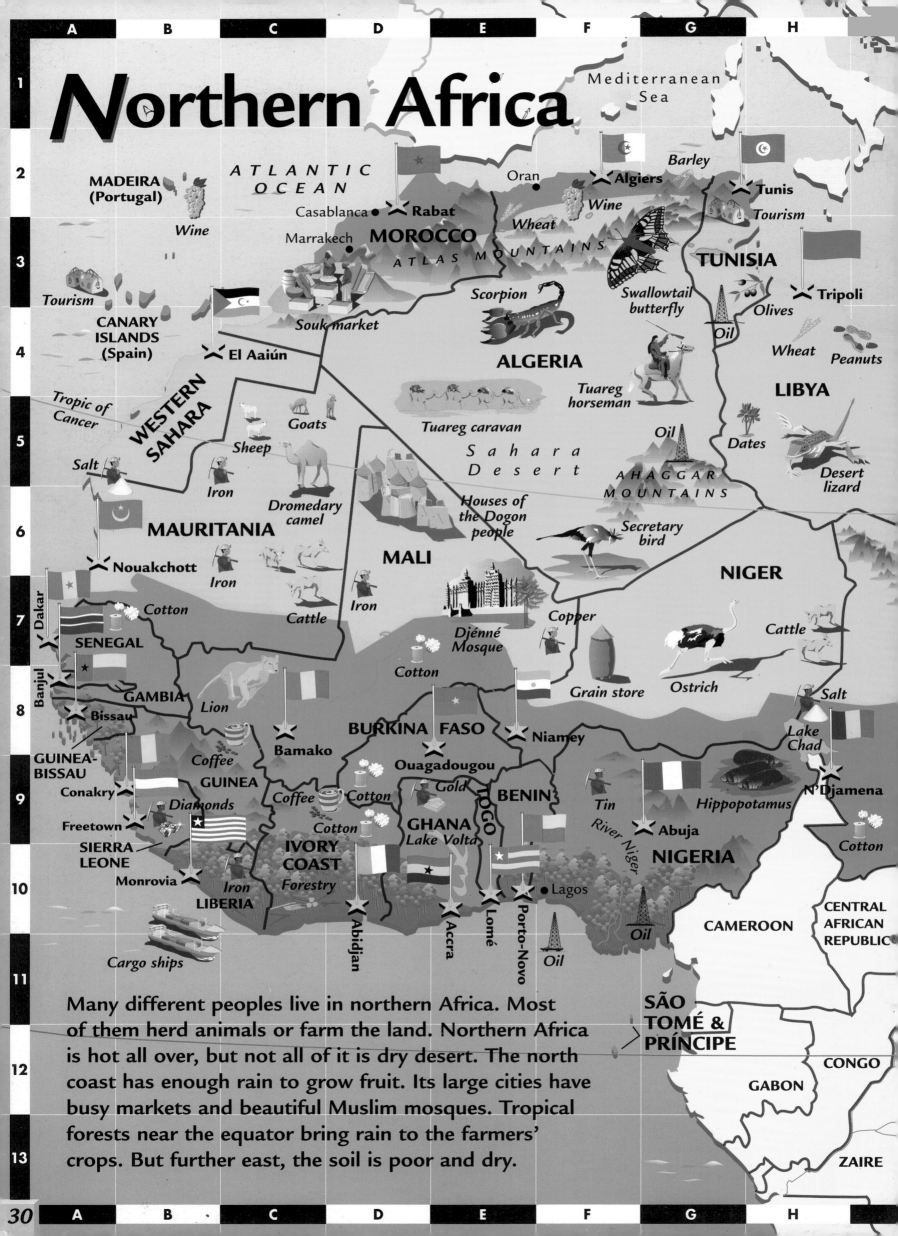

Northern Africa

Many different peoples live in northern Africa. Most of them herd animals or farm the land. Northern Africa is hot all over, but not all of it is dry desert. The north coast has enough rain to grow fruit. Its large cities have busy markets and beautiful Muslim mosques. Tropical forests near the equator bring rain to the farmers' crops. But further east, the soil is poor and dry.

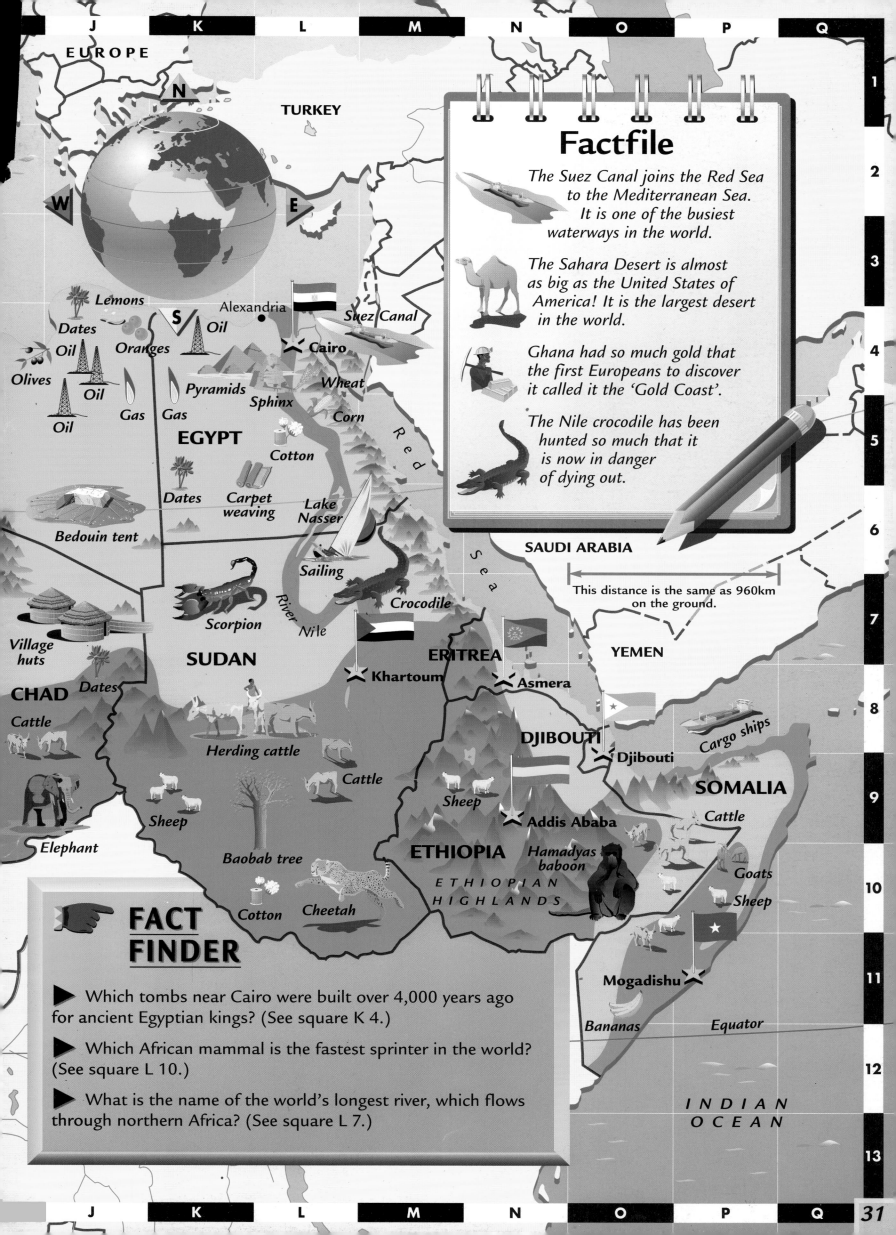

EUROPE

TURKEY

N

W S E

Factfile

The Suez Canal joins the Red Sea to the Mediterranean Sea. It is one of the busiest waterways in the world.

The Sahara Desert is almost as big as the United States of America! It is the largest desert in the world.

Ghana had so much gold that the first Europeans to discover it called it the 'Gold Coast'.

The Nile crocodile has been hunted so much that it is now in danger of dying out.

Lemons
Dates
Oil
Oranges
Oil
Olives
Oil
Oil
Gas
Gas
Alexandria
Oil
Suez Canal
Cairo
Pyramids
Sphinx
Wheat
Corn
Cotton
EGYPT
Dates
Carpet weaving
Lake Nasser
Sailing
Bedouin tent
Scorpion
River Nile
Crocodile

Red Sea

SAUDI ARABIA

This distance is the same as 960km on the ground.

Village huts
CHAD
Dates
Cattle
SUDAN
Khartoum
ERITREA
Asmera
YEMEN
Herding cattle
Cattle
DJIBOUTI
Djibouti
Cargo ships
Sheep
SOMALIA
Sheep
Addis Ababa
Cattle
Elephant
Baobab tree
ETHIOPIA
Hamadyas baboon
Goats
ETHIOPIAN HIGHLANDS
Sheep
Cotton
Cheetah

FACT FINDER

▶ Which tombs near Cairo were built over 4,000 years ago for ancient Egyptian kings? (See square K 4.)

▶ Which African mammal is the fastest sprinter in the world? (See square L 10.)

▶ What is the name of the world's longest river, which flows through northern Africa? (See square L 7.)

Mogadishu
Bananas
Equator
INDIAN OCEAN

Southern Africa

Southern Africa is a vast land of grasslands, rainforests, mountains and deserts. The plains of Kenya and Tanzania are famous for their huge herds of animals. Further west, in the rainforests, there are gorillas, monkeys and tropical birds. Many different peoples live in small villages, but the cities are growing. Many countries mine copper and gold. Some mine diamonds too.

Factfile

Southern Africa is home to the black rhino and the mountain gorilla, two of the world's most endangered animals.

Southern Africa has large areas of rainforest. Altogether, nearly one quarter of the world's forests grow in southern Africa.

Three-quarters of the world's diamonds are mined in southern Africa.

This distance is the same as 725km on the ground.

Tropic of Cancer

N
W E
S

NE

Equator

NIGERIA
Yams
Coffee

CHAD

CAMEROON
Forestry
Yaoundé
Oil
Malabo
EQUATORIAL GUINEA

Oil
Libreville
GABON
Forestry

Oil
CABINDA (Angola)
Oil
Brazzaville
CONGO
Forestry
Kinshasa

CENTRAL AFRICAN REPUBLIC
Cassava
Yams
Forestry
Bangui
Diamonds
Cotton
Crocodile

SUDAN

ETHIOPIA

SOMALIA

KENYA
Office blocks
Nairobi
Tea
Flamingoes

UGANDA
Kampala
Coffee
Lake Victoria
Coffee

Chimpanzee
River Zaire
Mountain gorilla
Coffee
R
Kigali
RWANDA
Bujumbura
BURUNDI
Lake Tanganyika

ZAIRE
Okapi
Dug-out canoes
Forestry
River Kasai
Cassava
African grey parrot
Diamonds

Mt Kilimanjaro
Elephants
Balloon safaris
Dodoma
Coffee

Tourism
Zanzibar Island
Dar es Salaam
Sardines
SEYCHELLES

32

INDIAN OCEAN

COMOROS

Teardrop butterfly fish

Chameleon

MAYOTTE (France)

Sea horses

MAURITIUS

RÉUNION (France)

MADAGASCAR

Coffee

Ring-tailed lemur

Antananarivo

Baobab tree

Rice

Polka dot grouper fish

Sugar cane

Millet

Herding cattle

Bananas

Forestry

MALAWI

Farming with hand tools

Shrimp

Cashew nuts

Humpback whale

MOZAMBIQUE

Lake Nyasa

TANZANIA

Coffee

Lilongwe

Harare

Cotton

Maputo

Mbabane

Giraffe

Lusaka

ZIMBABWE

Ruins of Great Zimbabwe

SWAZILAND

Cargo ships

Copper

Tobacco

Gold

Cotton

Pretoria

LESOTHO

Durban

Lobster

Copper

ZAMBIA

Victoria Falls

Maseru

Cargo ships

Black rhino

Diamonds

Tobacco

River Zambezi

Diamonds

Johannesburg

Coal

Corn

Zebra

Hippopotamus

Gold

Gold

Diamonds

Gold

Cargo ships

ANGOLA

Coffee

Luanda

Weaverbird

Lion

BOTSWANA

Kalahari Desert

Gaborone

REPUBLIC OF SOUTH AFRICA

Cattle

Apples

Cattle

Diamonds

Oranges

Wine

Village of Ovambo people

NAMIBIA

Meerkats

Windhoek

Cattle

Ostrich

Cape Town

Cape of Good Hope

ATLANTIC OCEAN

Anchovies

Diamonds

Welwitschia plant

Namib Desert

River Orange

Table Mountain

Cargo ships

Tropic of Capricorn

Right whale

Cargo ships

FACT FINDER

▲ What is the name of the largest lake in Africa and the second largest lake in the world? (See square H 7.)

▲ Which African mountain is close to the equator, but is so high that it is always covered in snow? (See square H 8.)

▲ Which African tree can store more than five hundred bathtubs of water in its trunk? (See square K 14.)

Southern Asia

Southern Asia stretches from the Himalayan Mountains in the north of India to the island of Sri Lanka in the south. The weather is mostly hot and dry, although for several months there are heavy rains. More than a billion people live in southern Asia. Most people live in villages and farm the land, but many are beginning to move to the cities. The cities are a mixture of old and new, with modern buildings next to ancient temples and palaces. The busy streets are packed with cars, trucks and lorries, but also with bullock carts and elephants.

👉 FACT FINDER

▲ Which white marble temple, decorated with precious stones, was built in the 17th century by an Indian emperor as a burial place for his wife? (See square G 8.)

▲ In India, which animal is used to help people with heavy work such as moving timber? (See square F 11.)

▲ What are Pakistan, Afghanistan and India all famous for weaving? (See squares C 6, C 9 and F 7.)

▲ In India, which three-wheeled vehicle that looks a little like a bicycle is often used to carry people from one place to another? (See square I 10.)

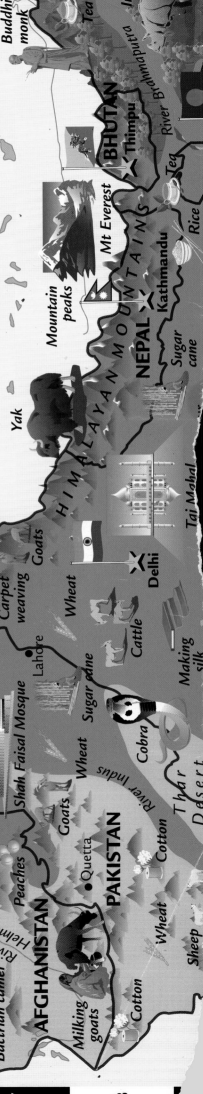

TURKMENISTAN

UZBEKISTAN

TAJIKISTAN

AFGHANISTAN

Blue Mosque

Carpet weaving

Cattle

Kabul

Bactrian camel

River Helmand

Rubies

Peaches

Goats

Quetta

Cotton

Wheat

Cobra

Thar Desert

River Indus

PAKISTAN

Cotton

Wheat

Sheep

Making silk

Cattle

Sugar cane

Wheat

Lahore

Shah Faisal Mosque

Islamabad

Carpet weaving

Wheat

Goats

KARAKORAM RANGE

Snow leopard

Yak

CHINA

Delhi

Taj Mahal

HIMALAYAN MOUNTAINS

Mountain peaks

Mt Everest

Sugar cane

Kathmandu

NEPAL

Rice

Tea

Thimpu

BHUTAN

Buddhist monk

Tea

Oil

River Brahmaputra

Indian rhino

Milking goats

Factfile

More films are made in southern Asia than anywhere else in the world. India makes over 800 films a year.

The mountains of southern Asia are home to the snow leopard, one of the world's most endangered animals.

Southern Asia is the world's largest producer of tea.

Eastern Asia

Eastern Asia is made up of China, Mongolia, Japan, North and South Korea, Taiwan and Hong Kong. It is a vast land with mountains and deserts in the north and west. Most people live further east, where there is more rain and good farmland. China is a huge country. Many people are farmers and live in the countryside. In Japan, most people live in cities. They work in factories and offices.

RUSSIA

This distance is the same as 450km on the ground.

Goats

Red deer

ALTAI MOUNTAINS

TIEN SHAN MOUNTAINS

Ulan Bator

Yurt

M O N G

Coal

Wolf

Copper

Gobi

Oil

Cotton

Goats

Iron

Sheep

Bactrian camel

Rice

Wheat

Sand grouse

Wild horses

Cotton

T a k l a   M a k a n   D e s e r t

Sheep

Wild horses

Cotton

Oil

Sheep

Great Wall of China

PAKISTAN

Gas

Vulture

Cotton

K2 (Mt Godwin Austen)

Tai Chi exercises

Salt mining

Snow leopard

TIBET

Calligraphy

Wild boar

C H I N A

INDIA

HIMALAYAN MOUNTAINS

Yak

Cattle

Goats

Sheep

Buddhist monk

Pigs

Chengdu

Mountain peaks

Potala Palace

Mt Everest

Great Buddha

BHUTAN

INDIA

N

MYANMAR

Stone forest

W

E

Tobacco

S

Tea

LAOS

THAILAND

FACT FINDER

▶ Which ancient exercises do many Chinese people perform every morning to keep themselves healthy? (See E 7.)

▶ Which wall is over 3,400km long and was built over 500 years ago to protect China from northern invaders? (See square H 6.)

▶ What is the name of the tent travelling herders in Mongolia live in to protect themselves from the heat and cold of the plains? (See square G 3.)

Factfile

In Tibet, one person in every five is a Buddhist monk, or lama.

More people live in China than in any other country. It contains about one fifth of all the people in the world.

Japan catches the most fish in the world. Along with rice, it is the main food eaten by the Japanese people.

South-east Asia

TAIWAN

Scuba diving

CHINA

Tropic of Cancer

Clown fish

Coral

Stilt house

South China Sea

LUZON

Coral

Wild boar

MYANMAR

Coal

Water buffalo

Hanoi

LAOS

Tiger

Copper

Manila

PHILIP

Working elephant

Rice

River Irrawaddy

Vientiane

THAILAND

River Mekong

VIETNAM

Making silk

Cargo ships

Coral

Herring

Silver

Floating market

Rice

Cassava

Anchovies

Gold

Yangon

Bangkok

Corn

Sardines

INDIAN OCEAN

Angkor Wat

Ho Chi Minh City

Phnom Penh

CAMBODIA

Pearls

Rice

Oil

Reef sharks

Lobster

Tourism

Gas

Oil

Tuna

BRUNEI

Bandar Seri Begawan

Making rubber

Leatherback turtle

Rice

Polka dot grouper fish

Malayan tapir

Iron

MALAYSIA

Forestry

Orang-utan

Coral

Tourism Kuala Lumpur

Office blocks

SINGAPORE

BORNEO

Gas

Forestry

Oil

Volcanoes

Oil

SUMATRA

Cargo ships

INDO

Gas

Volcanoes

Orchid

Volcanoes

Rafflesia flower

Jakarta JAVA

Tea

Sea horses

Teardrop butterfly fish

Coral

South-east Asia is made up of a narrow strip of land and thousands of small islands. The area has high mountains, tropical forests and river valleys. The weather is hot and wet all year round. Many of the people are farmers, who grow rice and corn for food, and rubber and coffee to sell. But the cities are growing, and more people are finding work in factories and offices.

Factfile

Rubber is made from the sap of the rubber tree. South-east Asia produces over three-quarters of the world's rubber.

There are more active volcanoes in south-east Asia than in any other area of the world. The ash left behind from volcanic eruptions helps to make the soil good for farming.

The country of Indonesia is made up of over 13,000 islands. It is the biggest chain of islands in the world and has the world's fourth largest population.

This distance is the same as 800km on the ground.

Bicycle rickshaw

PINES

Coconuts
MINDANAO

Outrigger fishing boat

NORTH PACIFIC OCEAN

Equator

Tuna

Bird of paradise

Coconuts

Sponge

Gas Oil

IRIAN JAYA (Indonesia)

Coconuts

PAPUA NEW GUINEA

MALUKU

Shrimp

Bananas

Cloves

Tree kangaroo

Port Moresby

Echidna

SULAWESI

Flying lizard

Crab

Coffee

Humpback whale

Manta ray

NESIA

Komodo dragon   FLORES   TIMOR

BALI   SUMBA

Shrimp

N

E

Tourism

W

AUSTRALIA

S

Dolphins

Tropic of Capricorn

Australia, New Zealand
and the Pacific Islands

The Pacific Ocean is dotted with thousands of islands. Many people live in villages and grow crops or hunt for fish. Australia is an island too, but it is so big that it is a continent. Most Australians live in cities or farm land near the coast. A lot of Australia is hot and dry, but it has mountains and rainforests too. It also has animals and plants that are not found anywhere else.

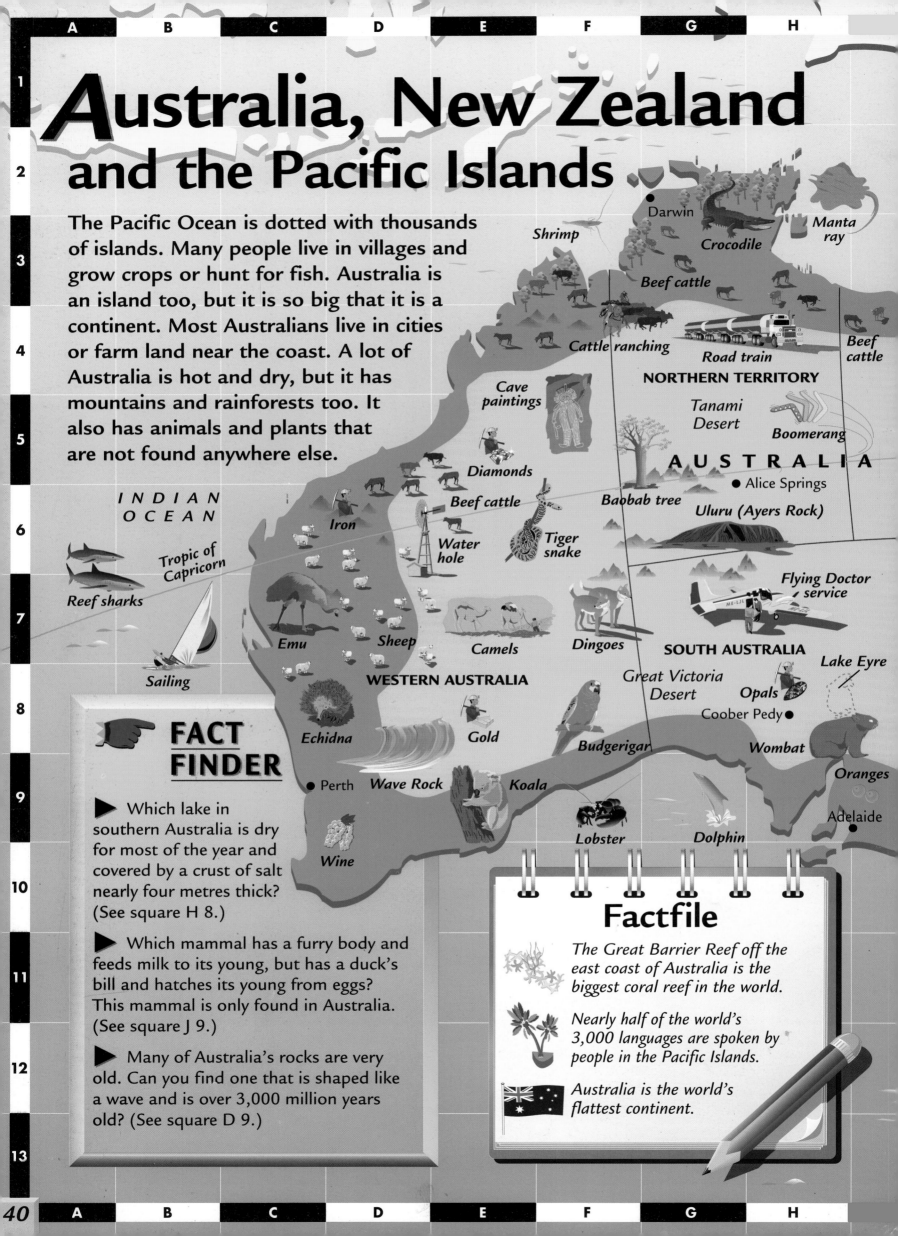

INDIAN OCEAN

Shrimp

Darwin

Crocodile

Manta ray

Beef cattle

Cattle ranching

Road train

NORTHERN TERRITORY

Beef cattle

Cave paintings

Tanami Desert

Boomerang

Diamonds

A U S T R A L I A

Beef cattle

Baobab tree

● Alice Springs

Uluru (Ayers Rock)

Iron

Water hole

Tiger snake

Tropic of Capricorn

Flying Doctor service

Reef sharks

Emu

Sheep

Camels

Dingoes

SOUTH AUSTRALIA

Lake Eyre

Sailing

WESTERN AUSTRALIA

Great Victoria Desert

Opals

Coober Pedy ●

Wombat

Echidna

Gold

Budgerigar

Oranges

● Perth

Wave Rock

Koala

Adelaide ●

Wine

Lobster

Dolphin

FACT FINDER

▶ Which lake in southern Australia is dry for most of the year and covered by a crust of salt nearly four metres thick? (See square H 8.)

▶ Which mammal has a furry body and feeds milk to its young, but has a duck's bill and hatches its young from eggs? This mammal is only found in Australia. (See square J 9.)

▶ Many of Australia's rocks are very old. Can you find one that is shaped like a wave and is over 3,000 million years old? (See square D 9.)

Factfile

The Great Barrier Reef off the east coast of Australia is the biggest coral reef in the world.

Nearly half of the world's 3,000 languages are spoken by people in the Pacific Islands.

Australia is the world's flattest continent.

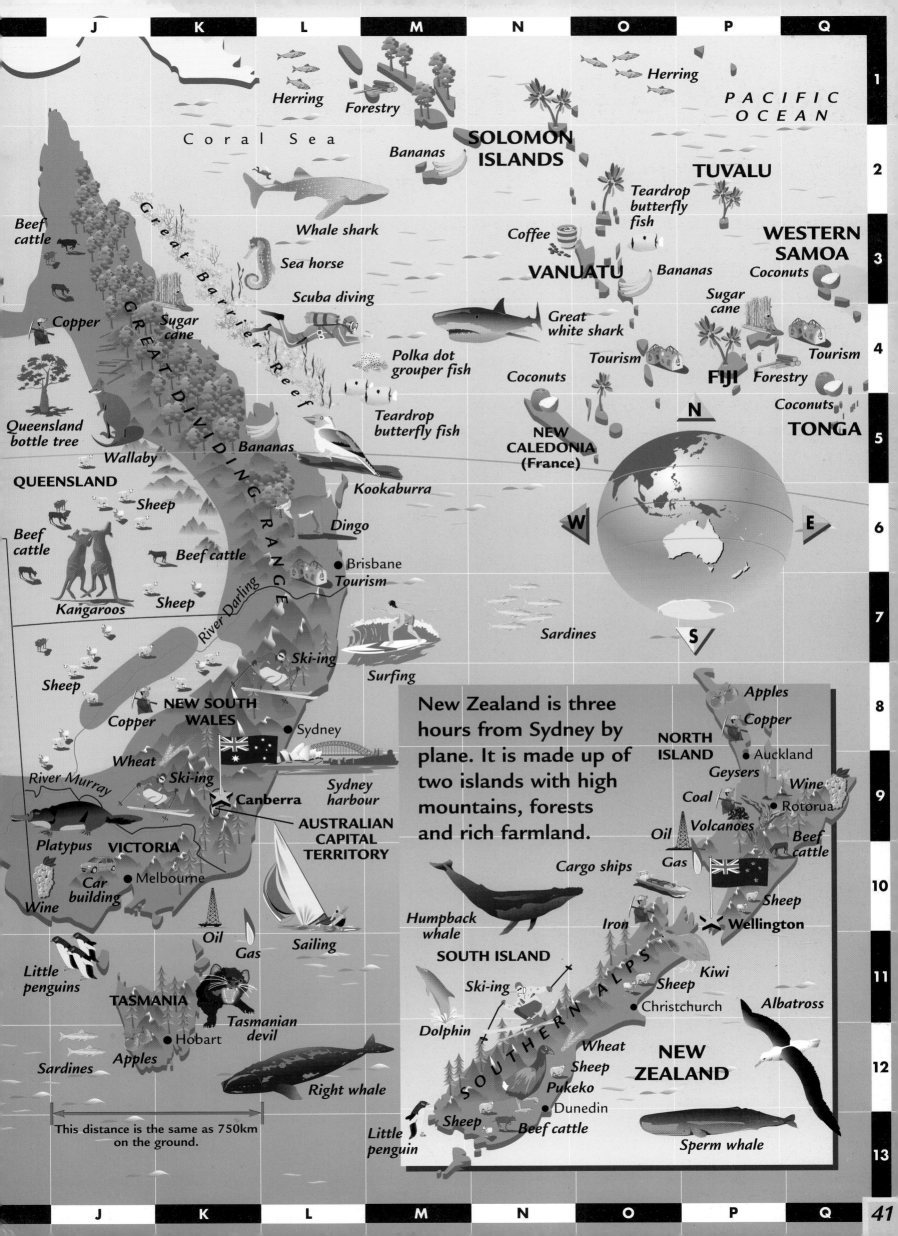

1

PACIFIC OCEAN

Herring

Forestry

Herring

Coral Sea

Bananas

SOLOMON ISLANDS

TUVALU

2

Beef cattle

Teardrop butterfly fish

WESTERN SAMOA

Whale shark

Coffee

Coconuts

3

Copper

Sea horse

Bananas

VANUATU

Sugar cane

Sugar cane

Scuba diving

Great white shark

Tourism

Tourism

4

Polka dot grouper fish

Coconuts

FIJI

Forestry

Queensland bottle tree

Teardrop butterfly fish

NEW CALEDONIA (France)

Coconuts

TONGA

5

Wallaby

Bananas

N

QUEENSLAND

Kookaburra

6

Sheep

Dingo

Beef cattle

Brisbane

W

E

Beef cattle

Beef cattle

Tourism

Kangaroos

Sheep

Sheep

Sardines

S

7

Sheep

Ski-ing

Surfing

8

NEW SOUTH WALES

Apples

NORTH ISLAND

Copper

Copper

Sydney

New Zealand is three hours from Sydney by plane. It is made up of two islands with high mountains, forests and rich farmland.

Auckland

Wheat

River Murray

Ski-ing

Geysers

Wine

9

Canberra

Sydney harbour

Coal

Rotorua

Platypus

VICTORIA

AUSTRALIAN CAPITAL TERRITORY

Volcanoes

Oil

Beef cattle

Car building

Melbourne

Cargo ships

Gas

10

Wine

Humpback whale

Iron

Sheep

Oil

Gas

Sailing

SOUTH ISLAND

Wellington

Little penguins

11

Ski-ing

Kiwi

TASMANIA

Sheep

Tasmanian devil

Dolphin

Christchurch

Albatross

Hobart

Wheat

NEW ZEALAND

12

Sardines

Apples

Sheep

Right whale

Pukeko

This distance is the same as 750km on the ground.

Dunedin

Little penguin

Sheep

Beef cattle

Sperm whale

13

Gazetteer

On these pages, you can discover interesting facts about the world. Look up the names of the places in the index and find out where they are on the maps in this atlas.

Where in the world is...

...the hottest place?
Dallol in Ethiopia, which has an average temperature of 34°C (94°F).

In Dallol, you could fry an egg on a sun-baked rock.

...the coldest place?
Vostock in Antarctica. The lowest temperature ever recorded was -89°C (-128°F), which is over three times as cold as inside a deep freeze.

...the wettest place?
Mawsynram in India, where nearly 12m of rain falls each year. This is enough to cover a three-storey building.

...the driest place?
Atacama Desert in Chile, where it has rained only a few times in the last 400 years.

Which country is the...

...biggest country?
Russia, which is 17,075,400sq km.

...smallest country?
Vatican City, which is 0.44sq km.

If Russia were the size of a soccer pitch, the Vatican City would be the size of a small stamp.

...emptiest country?
Mongolia, which has a huge desert and high mountains. There are only a few towns which are far apart.

...most crowded country?
Monaco, which is a tiny country in Europe. It has an orchestra larger than its army.

Where is the...

...highest mountain in the world?
Mount Everest in the Himalayas in Nepal. It is 8,848m high, which is over nine times as tall as the highest waterfall in the world.

8,848m

...highest waterfall in the world?
Angel Falls in Venezuela. It has a total drop of 979m. It is over twice as high as the tallest building in North America.

979m

...highest building in North America?
Sears Tower, USA. It is 443m tall, nearly four times taller than the tallest geyser in the world.

443m

...highest geyser in the world?
Steamboat Geyser, USA. It has reached 115.85m, slightly taller than the tallest tree in the world.

115.85m

...highest tree in the world?
A redwood tree in California, USA. It is 111.56m, over 40 times taller than the tallest person in the world.

111.56m

Who was the world's tallest person?
An American called Robert Pershing Wadlow was the world's tallest person. He was 2.72m tall.

FACT FINDER

Find these record-breaking places in the atlas.

▶ The highest mountain (page 34, square J 8)

▶ The tallest waterfall (page 20, square E 4)

▶ The longest river (page 31, square L 7)

▶ The driest place (page 21, square E 9)

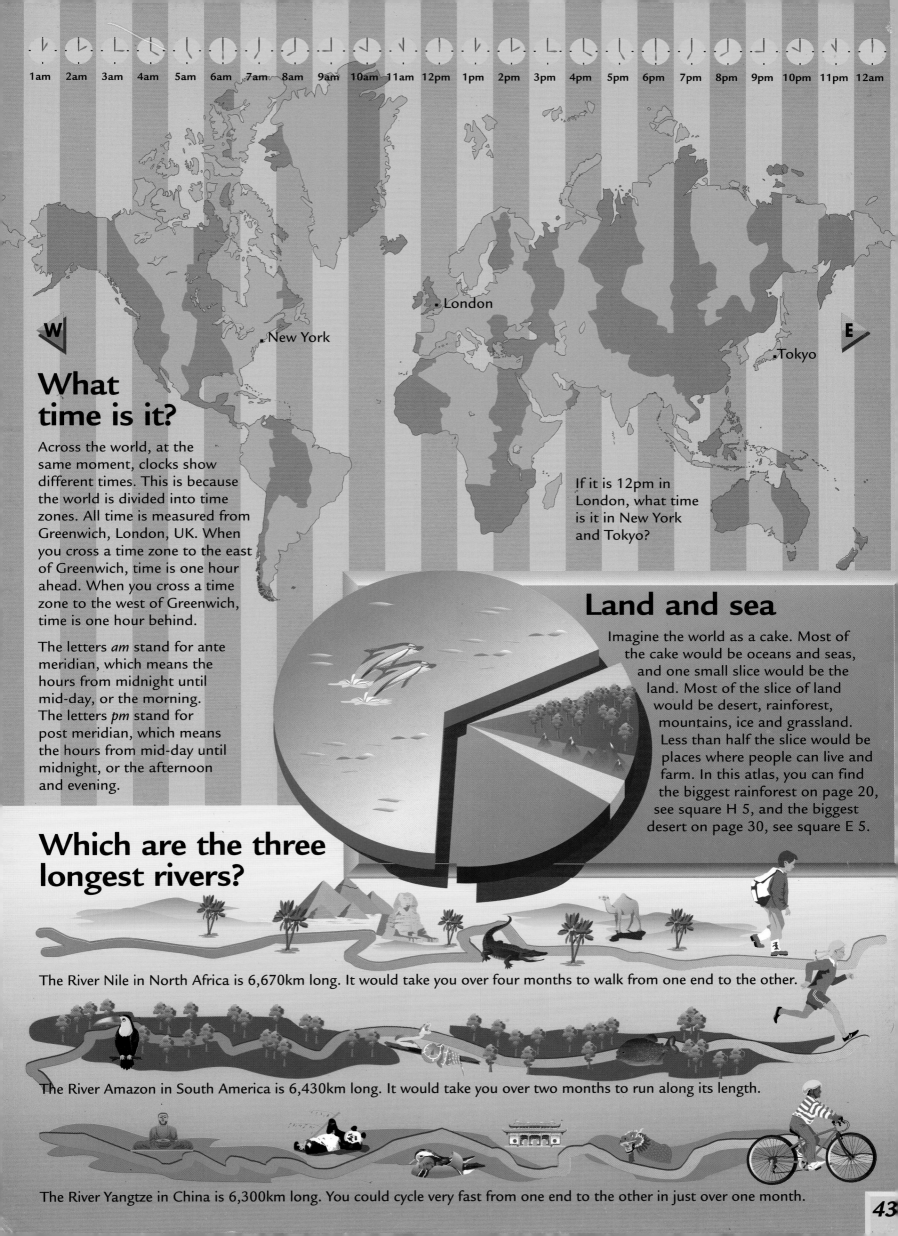

1am 2am 3am 4am 5am 6am 7am 8am 9am 10am 11am 12pm 1pm 2pm 3pm 4pm 5pm 6pm 7pm 8pm 9pm 10pm 11pm 12am

W

London

New York

E

Tokyo

What time is it?

Across the world, at the same moment, clocks show different times. This is because the world is divided into time zones. All time is measured from Greenwich, London, UK. When you cross a time zone to the east of Greenwich, time is one hour ahead. When you cross a time zone to the west of Greenwich, time is one hour behind.

The letters *am* stand for ante meridian, which means the hours from midnight until mid-day, or the morning. The letters *pm* stand for post meridian, which means the hours from mid-day until midnight, or the afternoon and evening.

If it is 12pm in London, what time is it in New York and Tokyo?

Land and sea

Imagine the world as a cake. Most of the cake would be oceans and seas, and one small slice would be the land. Most of the slice of land would be desert, rainforest, mountains, ice and grassland. Less than half the slice would be places where people can live and farm. In this atlas, you can find the biggest rainforest on page 20, see square H 5, and the biggest desert on page 30, see square E 5.

Which are the three longest rivers?

The River Nile in North Africa is 6,670km long. It would take you over four months to walk from one end to the other.

The River Amazon in South America is 6,430km long. It would take you over two months to run along its length.

The River Yangtze in China is 6,300km long. You could cycle very fast from one end to the other in just over one month.

Index

This index lists all the places on the maps in this atlas. The page number tells you which map to go to and the grid reference tells you where the place is on the map. You can find out how to use grid references on page 9.